SUPERVISING PEOPLE

By the Same Author

HANDBOOK OF PERSONNEL MANAGEMENT

TRAINING EMPLOYEES

SELECTING AND INDUCTING EMPLOYEES

SUPERVISING PEOPLE

by

GEORGE D. HALSEY

Personnel Officer, Third District Farm Credit Administration
formerly
General Superintendent, Bloomingdale Brothers
Personnel Director, Woodward & Lothrop
Employment Manager, Cincinnati Milling Machine Co.

REVISED EDITION

HARPER & BROTHERS PUBLISHERS

NEW YORK

SUPERVISING PEOPLE

G-C

Library of Congress catalog card number: 53-8537

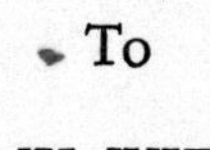

To

MY WIFE

CONTENTS

PREFACE
TO THE REVISED EDITION

Considerable progress in the art of supervising people has been made since the first edition of this book was published. Fundamental principles have, of course, remained unchanged; but understanding of these principles and skill in applying them to everyday problems of supervision have increased greatly.

A new chapter discusses recent developments in two-way communication. Other new material has been added, especially to the chapters discussing the important subjects of employee merit rating and the use of tests in the selection of employees. Changes have been made also in several other chapters in order to bring the discussions up to date.

As I have reviewed the large amount of material available and selected that which I thought should be included in this revision, I have kept in mind always that this book is intended primarily for supervisors—foremen in shops and mills, section heads in offices, assistant buyers and floor managers in retail stores—the men and women directly in charge of the workers and finally responsible for whether or not each individual's work is well done. And, since supervisors are busy people, it deals primarily with the practical aspects of supervision—what have been the problems of other supervisors and how they have solved these problems. Basic principles and theories are discussed; but primarily for the light they shed on why one method of supervision is better than another.

The book is so arranged that it can be used either as a text for groups studying the art of supervising people or for individual study. Chapters are of such a length that each will serve as a basis for discussion at one or two meetings, or as an evening's reading.

Each chapter deals with a separate phase of the subject of supervision and each is reasonably independent of the others so that, if it is desired to arrange a short series of meetings, this may be done by selecting the chapters dealing with those phases of supervision of greatest interest to the group in attendance. Even for a short series of meetings, however, it is suggested that the material discussed in Chapter III (*Understanding Human Behavior*) be included as an introduction to a discussion of the more specific topics.

Following each chapter are carefully selected references to other books and articles for those who wish to study the subject more fully.

The suggestions on how best to supervise people made in this book are by no means the product of one person's mind. Many people have through the years contributed to their development. Some of the ideas have come from books, but many more have come from watching and talking with successful supervisors.

It has been an important part of my work for more than thirty years to organize and lead groups of shop and foundry foremen and supervisors in offices, banks, and stores in discussions of the important question of how they could do better the job of supervising the people under them. Early in that experience I formed the habit of asking the members of the groups to tell me what they believed to be the best way to do this or that, rather than to attempt first to tell them. I have learned much from these men and women. In fact, to a large degree, they have written this book.

With permission of the publishers, use is made in several instances of material which appeared first in articles in the magazines *Your Life* and *Your Personality*.

Dr. Ordway Tead read the manuscript several times during its preparation and made many helpful suggestions.

My wife and son have been most helpful in that they have supplemented my own viewpoint with that of those whose problems in supervision are principally in the home, in church and social groups, and in college.

Comments and suggestions for improvement from readers will be most sincerely appreciated.

GEORGE D. HALSEY

SUPERVISING PEOPLE

CHAPTER I

What Is Supervision?

A COMMITTEE was studying the problem of how to cut down the number of accidents in a large plant. No one of the recent accidents had been serious; but the total of the time lost was serious. Various suggestions were offered—added safety devices, bulletin boards, meetings, new rules, rewards, penalties. But all these things had been tried before with only limited and temporary success. Finally one man said, and all agreed, "It seems to me that this is really a problem of supervision—a problem for the foremen to handle with their men."

In a large mail-order house the poor quality of letters being sent out was a source of serious concern to the management. Not only were the typing and arrangement not neat, but often the tone of the letters was such that customers were offended. And yet considerable money had been spent in preparing a "style manual" and copies had been given each dictator and transcriber. Here too, after a discussion of possible bulletin board notices, purchase of more manuals, rules, rewards, and penalties, the decision was the same as in the shop—the problem was one of improving the quality of supervision.

And so it is with almost every situation that calls for cooperation and continuous attention to detail by rank-and-file employees—if supervision is good, there is no problem, everything moves smoothly; if supervision is poor, nothing that is done seems to have the desired effect.

The solution to practically all such problems is just this: *improve the quality of your supervision.*

But what is this thing we call supervision?

The best answer to that question I have ever heard was that

given a few years ago by a group of foremen at the first of a series of meetings being held to discuss the question of how they could improve the quality of their supervision.

The discussion leader opened with the comment that, since the group would be discussing the subject of supervision for several meetings, it might be well first to define the word. So he asked the group to do this.

"I don't know that I can give the entire definition," one foreman replied, "but I can start it. Certainly it has to do with something we the foremen and supervisors must do *in order to get the people under our supervision to do their assigned tasks properly;* but I don't know exactly how to define just *what* we must do or *how* we must do it."

"That is an excellent start even if it isn't the full definition," replied the leader. "Let's put that much on the board. As you say, supervision is doing something to people in order to cause them to do their assigned tasks properly. We haven't decided on *what* that something is or just *how* we are to do it, so we shall leave blank spaces to be filled in later. Here is about how the definition will look this far:

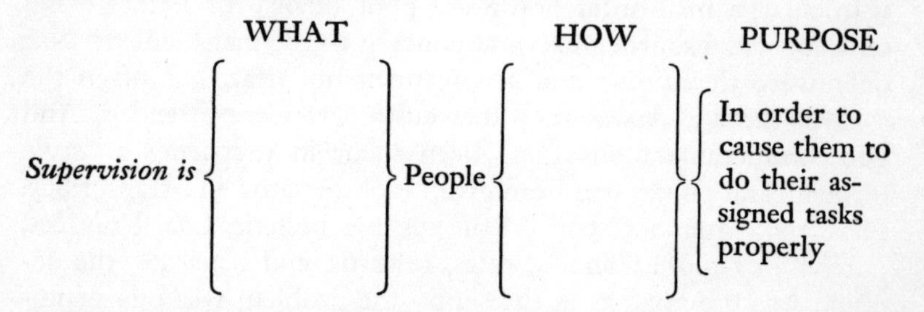

"Now that is done, let's consider first what we must do to people in order to get them to do properly the work we have assigned to them. What is the first thing?" continued the leader.

"First of all we must select the right person for each job," someone suggested promptly. "No amount of anything we can do will make a person who is not fitted for his work do that work properly."

So the word "selecting" was written in under WHAT.

"Next, I should think, would be explaining the importance of the work so as to make the employee interested and teaching him how to do it if he doesn't already know," was the next suggestion.

"And that should probably be followed by measuring the performance and rating it in comparison with some standard to be sure that a good job of teaching has been done," quickly suggested another foreman. "And, where teaching has not proved effective and work is not being done properly, further teaching or correction will be necessary. All of these are, it seems to me, part of the foreman's job—part of supervision."

Five words were added to the list—"interesting," "teaching," "measuring," "rating," "correcting"—and the group leader asked if that didn't about finish it.

"No," replied one of the older foremen. "Even after we have done all these things as carefully as we can, there will always be some people who cannot or will not do the work as it should be done. They must be eliminated by transfer or dismissal. These aren't the most pleasant parts of supervision but are, I believe, necessary ones."

The group agreed and the word "eliminating" was added.

"We must not forget one important thing—seeing that the employee who does do a good job is commended and properly rewarded either by promotion, salary increase, or in some other effective manner," was the final suggestion for this part of the definition.

Two more words—"commending" and "rewarding"—were added, and the definition on the board looked like this:

	WHAT		HOW	PURPOSE
Supervision is	Selecting Interesting Teaching Measuring Rating Correcting Eliminating Commending Rewarding	People		In order to cause them to do their assigned tasks properly

"Now, for the best success in supervising people, *how* shall we do all these things?" continued the discussion leader.

"With conditions as they are right now, I think patience is

about the most important quality which must be in everything we do, so I would suggest that as the first word," was the first suggestion made by a foreman whose department had recently expanded to several times its original size.

"Patience is, as you say, especially important right now with so many people entirely new to our type of work coming into the organization, and it is important even in more normal times; so, if there are no objections, we will put 'patiently' at the head of the *How* list," replied the leader. "How about it, shall we leave it at the head of the list?"

"I believe fairness is even more important than patience," replied one of the men. "In fact, I think it is the most important of all qualities necessary for success in supervision, so I suggest that it be put first on the list."

"Bill is right on that," said the foreman who had suggested patience. "I know I can forgive almost anything in a man I work for, including impatience; but if he shows favoritism or is deliberately unfair in any of his dealings with me, I am through. So I am in favor of putting fairness at the head of the list."

All agreed, and "fairly" was put first and "patiently" second.

"One thing is important, especially with women workers," commented a woman supervisor, "and that is the manner in which things are done. For example, when correcting a person it is important to do it as privately as possible so as not to cause unnecessary embarrassment. Such little personal things as remembering and using names, remembering to ask about someone who is ill or about a son who is away in school or in the army, and not forgetting to say 'Good morning' promptly and pleasantly are most important. There are a host of such little acts which show thoughtfulness and consideration for the feelings of others which mean much to women workers. Perhaps 'tact' is the one word which most nearly means all of that."

"Men like those things, too," added one of the foremen from the foundry. "Perhaps they don't show their feelings quite so plainly as women workers do; but they feel just as keenly anything which takes away from their feeling of self-respect. I have known more than one man to quit a good job with the statement that he could not keep his self-respect and continue to work for that 'so-and-so'! Perhaps the tact necessary in the foundry and forging departments is of a little rougher variety than that necessary in dealing with women in the assembly department and office; but it is the same inside—just being considerate of the feelings of people."

So "tactfully" was added to the list.

"I have been looking at the word 'properly' at the end," one of the men said, thoughtfully, after the definition was completed this far. "It seems to me that, for the definition to be complete, we should explain just what we mean by properly. I can suggest two words, 'skillfully' and 'accurately'; probably there are others."

"That is an excellent thought," commented the leader, "and we will erase the word 'properly' and put a bracket at the end, and start off with the words, 'skillfully' and 'accurately.' Are there other suggestions?"

The words "intelligently," "enthusiastically," and "completely" were suggested.

"Now, does that have our definition complete? Is there anything else that should be added?" asked the leader.

"There is one more thing which may or may not belong in the definition of supervision," one supervisor replied. It probably belongs in the *What* column if anywhere. I am thinking about the supervisor's responsibility for making each person as congenial as possible with everyone else in the section so that working here will prove to be a satisfying social experience as well as a means of making a livelihood. I don't mean necessarily that every supervisor should arrange picnics for his people every so often, although that might be a good thing; but he can encourage little social acts, if nothing more than checkers or horseshoe pitching at noon. Also, he can try to get to the bottom of minor frictions between individuals and try to correct these. But I cannot get that down to less than three words, 'promote congeniality among.' "

"That certainly is an idea worth considering, and if it belongs in it should go in no matter how many words it takes," replied the leader. "What do the members of the group think? Is that a part of supervision?"

"I think it is, but I believe there should be a caution," replied an office supervisor. "People can become too congenial and want to be visiting and talking about last Saturday's picnic instead of working. Some of even that is fine. It makes people happy on the job, and they work better; but the supervisor must know just how much of a good thing is enough. What we are probably after is to cause people to work together in friendly harmony, so couldn't we use the word 'harmonizing' to indicate how much promoting of congeniality we wish to do?"

All agreed, and that word was added. There were no further suggestions and the definition became:

	WHAT		HOW		PURPOSE
Supervision is	Selecting Interesting Teaching Measuring Rating Correcting Eliminating Commending Rewarding Harmonizing	People	Fairly Patiently Tactfully	In order to cause them to do their assigned tasks	Skillfully Accurately Intelligently Enthusiastically Completely

Supervision, then, is selecting the right person for each job; arousing in each person an interest in his work and teaching him how to do it; measuring and rating performance to be sure that teaching has been fully effective; administering correction where this is found necessary and transferring to more suitable work or dismissing those for whom this proves ineffective; commending whenever praise is merited and rewarding for good work; and, finally, fitting each person harmoniously into the working group —all done fairly, patiently, and tactfully so that each person is caused to do his work skillfully, accurately, intelligently, enthusiastically, and completely.

When we look at that definition—and it is an accurate statement of what every supervisor must do—we begin to realize just how important and how complex is this job of supervising people.

Is Supervision a Profession?

Perhaps the best way to answer that question is first to ask and answer another question: What is a profession? What requirements must be met by an occupation or calling before it can justly be classed as a profession?

Careful study of the definition of the word and of the distinctive features of those callings which are commonly accepted as professions seems to point to three requirements:

1. To follow the calling successfully one must be possessed of some special knowledge which requires considerable study and effort to obtain.
2. There must be certain standards, usually both ethical and technical, to which the members of the calling are expected to conform and usually do conform.
3. It must be a calling that is not purely commercial in that service to some cause or ideal is put higher than solely financial gain.

Does the supervision of people measure up to these requirements?

Certainly it does the first one. A thorough understanding of human nature and a knowledge of the techniques of supervision are essential to success and, for most of us, these are not obtained without considerable effort and study.

How well it measures up to the other requirements depends on just how well and how conscientiously we supervisors do our work.

Do we have and live up to any standard of ethics?

Such standards for supervisors have been prepared, and these are discussed in Chapter XXIV. More and more codes of ethics similar to this are being adopted by groups of supervisors, and more and more they are being lived up to.

Do we set service to the people under our supervision, and our loyalty to them, higher than mere financial gain?

In a great number of cases, yes; but is this general enough to justify calling our work a profession? I don't know.

But I do know that, as we set higher and higher standards for that part of our work which has to do with the supervision of people and do not consider it as merely an incidental part of our total job—the main qualification for which is our knowledge of mechanical processes, office techniques, or merchandising methods—the more will the supervision of people be recognized as truly a profession.

But, aren't supervisors "born, not made?"

We often hear the remark that no one can learn to be a good supervisor unless he is just naturally so, because "leaders are born, not made." But there is another familiar and probably more truthful saying: "Nine-tenths of genius is sweat."

It has been demonstrated time and time again that almost any person of normal intelligence and sincere desire to be of service to people can acquire considerable skill in the art of supervising people, if he will study its principles and methods and apply them thoughtfully, conscientiously, and persistently. The personality of the successful supervisor of people is made up of a number of qualities and these qualities are made effective through the use of certain definite techniques. I believe, too, that the qualities necessary to success in supervising people can be developed and that the required techniques can be taught and skill in their use made permanent by practice. I believe this because I have seen it done by both old and new supervisors, and seen their departments improve as they became better supervisors.

But there is one important fact that should be kept constantly in mind: Real skill in supervising people must be the resultant of sound and logical thinking, fair and considerate feeling toward people and a sympathetic understanding of people, and not merely the acting of a part. It cannot be assumed as one would put on a costume. It must be based on the possession of certain qualities of body, mind, feeling, and character which must either be inherent or be developed by self-training and self-discipline—not by acting.

As each principle and rule of supervision is developed, you will probably agree that it is true, because there is nothing radical or even especially new about any of them. Yet mere knowing and agreeing are of little or no value. The important questions for each to ask himself are, "Do I actually apply each of these principles each day in my work? *Could I cite examples to prove this if someone asked me to do so?*"

And in answering we must try to be as impersonal and objective as possible, *remembering that there is probably no phase of human activity where one is so likely to try to find good excuses for his weakness and lack of real skill as in the handling of people.*

Suggested Supplementary Reading on the Definition and Scope of Supervision

How to Train Supervisors, R. O. Beckman.

Section II—Outline No. 1, Responsibilities of a Supervisor or Foreman, and Outline No. 30, Broader Aspects of the Supervisor's Job.

Handbook of Personnel Management, George D. Halsey.

In Chapter XII there is a description of the supervisor's duties and responsibilities which is a composite of a number of such statements taken from material furnished the author by several organizations.

The Technique of Executive Control, E. H. Schell.

Chapter VII, Executive Duties.

Foremanship Training, Hugo Deimer.

Chapter II gives Frederick W. Taylor's analysis of the forman's job as presented to the American Society of Mechanical Engineers in 1903. This is one of the earliest attempts to list the foreman's responsibilities.

CHAPTER II

Six Qualities Important to Success as a Supervisor

I HAVE been a personnel director for twenty-five years. During that time it has been my good fortune to become well acquainted with many men and women who have started at the bottom and gone far up the ladder of achievement.

The nature of my duties has given me an unusual opportunity both to observe just how these executives went about their everyday work and to discuss with them the qualities they believed essential to success in supervising people—the qualities they wanted me to look for in the men and women we selected for admission to our supervisory training courses.

During that twenty-five years I have often had also the less pleasant task of talking with men and women whose work as supervisors was so unsatisfactory that they had to be warned that there must be some improvement if they expected to get ahead in the organization or even to keep the jobs they had.

As I talked with those who were successful and then with those who were not successful, often during the same day, I endeavored constantly to find out just what were the essential differences between the two groups. What do those who seem to be able to forge ahead in any business have that the majority in the same business do not have? Is it mostly "lucky breaks" or do they really "have something"?

A few years ago I prepared two lists of names, one of the twenty-five most successful supervisors I have known well and the other of the twenty-five men and women from the less successful group whose work and personalities I had an opportunity to study most closely. Then I compared the two groups by rating each individual on every quality I could think of which might have had a bearing on his or her success, not omitting even "lucky breaks" and being related to a big stockholder.

Six qualities stood out as being practically always well developed in the personality of each person who had achieved any marked degree of success. And definite lack of development in some of these six qualities was always evident in the personality of each person in the less successful group. The six qualities are: thoroughness, fairness, initiative, tact, enthusiasm, and emotional control.

On the list of less successful supervisors were included the names of several men who did achieve a considerable degree of temporary success; but who, when the test of the depression came, had failed, and have since been unable to stage a "comeback." In each of these cases, while there was strong development of three or four or even five of the six qualities, there was a definite weakness in one or more; and that weakness, when the strain came, was what had caused the whole structure to fail.

All this has firmly convinced me that, for any large measure of success—success that endures through hard times as well as good times—there must be an adequate and reasonably well-balanced development of all six qualities. *No one quality may safely be neglected.*

1. *Thoroughness*

While it is probable that no one of the six qualities can be called the most important, the one quality which I have found more consistently than any other to be well developed in the personalities of successful men and women, and lacking in those who have failed, is *thoroughness*—especially thoroughness in those things which, to the less successful, seem small and unimportant.

Time and time again I have seen some young supervisor come into the office of a senior executive with a recommendation, and have seen that senior executive examine the details and ask questions the supervisor could not answer because he had not taken time to get all of the facts. And they were important questions, questions the answers to which often showed the whole recommendation to be unsound. The supervisor would have known this, too, had he taken time to be thorough.

Perhaps the most important single thing I have learned from many years of close association with successful executives is that, in the long run, it takes less time to be thorough and to get your answer right from every viewpoint at the outset than it does to dash through and then often find it necessary to correct some serious mistake resulting from not having taken care of every detail.

And it is not alone in business that thoroughness is necessary for success. It is the lawyer who scarcely makes enough to pay rent for his desk space who asks only a few questions of his client, and then—cocks his hat on one side of his head and says: "That case is easy—it's already in the bag." The successful lawyer, the one who gets the fees we sometimes read about, looks into every detail of the case and spends hours in his library studying every possible angle on which some point could be made by the opposition.

Go to the office of the finest doctor in any city, and you will find there not the man who glances at you and says, "I know exactly what is wrong," and gives you a prescription, but the man who checks painstakingly every little thing that might have a bearing, and only then makes his decision.

Look back to the times when you have failed to accomplish something—something important—you had set out to do. Count how many of these times the failures have really been due, not to lack of knowledge, not to lack of experience or ability, not even to bad luck; but just to lack of thoroughness on your part, to the overlooking of some small detail.

Yes, the habit of thoroughness deserves first place on the list of qualities essential to success in any business or profession—and the profession of supervision is no exception.

Perhaps the best way to form this important habit of thoroughness is just to make up your mind that you will endeavor *always, before you call any job finished* to ask yourself these three simple questions:

Have I been *thorough?*

Have I obtained all the information I need?

Have I taken care of every necessary detail?

It has helped me to put these questions under the glass on my desk, near the telephone. When I reach for the phone to ask for an appointment to report on some matter to my chief, or when I start to call a supervisor about something on which I have only half information, I am reminded of the need for thoroughness and am often saved embarrassment.

This exact plan may not be the best for you. Possibly you will want to make some note on the flyleaf of a notebook or put it on every fourth or fifth page of your calendar pad. It matters not what system you use, the important thing in any attempt to form the habit of thoroughness is to keep yourself reminded. We *can* all be thorough, it takes no particular aptitude, or ability; and probably we all recognize the need for thoroughness. The only thing remaining is *to find some way to keep ourselves reminded*. Any thought and effort you may put into the task of finding the best method for yourself will be well spent.

2. *Fairness*

The quality considered most important by the majority of the groups of supervisors with whom I have discussed the subject and the quality the lack of which causes more employee grievances than any other is *fairness*. It is the only safe foundation for any lasting success in supervising people.

But most of us feel that we are fair in all our dealings with people and probably would resent any but a high rating on this quality. We might even consider wholly unnecessary any discussion of how best to develop fairness. And in the bigger things, there is little doubt but that we would get and deserve a high rating. We would not tell a deliberate falsehood about some employee either to save ourselves from criticism or to gain a promotion for some friend or relative; we would not deliberately claim personal credit for something someone under our supervision had done; nor are we knowingly guilty of any other major injustices. But when it comes to the little things which really count for so much, do we rate so high?

The actual achievement of fairness takes much more than the wish and intention to be fair.

Do we sometimes criticize an employee for some mistake when a careful inquiry would show that he has not been properly taught, that he is working with poor equipment, or that the light is poor and eyestrain with its resultant fatigue has been the cause?

Do we occasionally make careless comments about the ability of a person, comments which may cause others to form an adverse judgment, when our opinions are not based on thoughtful analysis of facts? Are we always extremely careful to base recommendations for salary increases on a fair and thoughtful measurement of real worth rather than on some chance circumstance, such as one recent favorable or unfavorable circumstance, an offer of another job, or the skill of the person in asking for an increase? Do we sometimes make promises to employees under our supervision, sincerely intending to keep these promises, but make no follow-up record so as to make sure the promises are kept?

For all of us the answers to all these questions will, occasionally at least, be "Yes."

It is only by careful and continuous watching to be fair in little things, supposedly unimportant things, that anyone can hope to achieve that high degree of intelligent fairness so necessary for success in supervision. There is no half way in fairness.

3. *Initiative*

Initiative is the capacity for assuming responsibility and for starting and doing things, the ability to carry through an undertaking without requiring too detailed supervision. It is that something which causes one man to stand out from the crowd in an emergency. It requires a combination of the three qualities, courage, self-confidence, and decisiveness, and also a certain degree of constructive inventiveness. *Courage* is that quality which enables one to meet dangers or difficulties with firmness and without wavering. It is not foolhardiness. It does not preclude the exercise of proper caution against taking unnecessary risks. It does not even mean absolute fearlessness. *Self-confidence* is faith in one's own strength or powers; belief in one's ability to accomplish a purpose, to do successfully the job he has undertaken. *Constructive inventiveness* is the ability to see possibilities for action in a situation, to devise ways to accomplish a desired purpose which have not been used before in the solution of that particular problem. It is knowing what to do. *Decisiveness* is the quality of deciding finally and without vacillation the questions which arise. "The leader must not only be decisive; he must impress his followers with the fact that a decision has been reached and that hesitation, vacillation, and questioning are over. He must *act* in a decided way and support his decision with a confident and courageous attitude. He must look decided."[1]

Perhaps the best way to approach the problem of developing initiative, if one does not already possess this important quality to a great enough degree, is first to consider what are the principal causes of fear, lack of self-confidence, and indecision. Four causes stand out:

Lack of knowledge. Ignorance and fear are almost synonymous. Virtually everything is simple if we but know all of the facts about it. The skilled electrician works fearlessly and, to the uninitiated observer, almost carelessly with wires and connections that would cause instant death if he were to touch the wrong one; but he has no fear, because he possesses an absolute knowledge of what will be the result of each action. He knows the right thing to do and what he may not do. Knowledge has vanquished fear.

So the first step toward self-confidence is: *Know your job.*

Lack of experience. Perhaps the safest foundation for courage in meeting important and serious situations is a background of having dealt successfully with a large number of relatively unimportant situations. Skill in making quick and accurate decisions in important matters, and courage and initiative in carrying out these decisions, can be gained by practice in making and carrying out decisions in less important matters. Practice in "taking the lead" can constantly be had in one's everyday contacts. For example: Find out what entertainment is available (knowledge), and reach your own decision in advance as to what would be an enjoyable thing for your group to do on Saturday afternoon. Then, when the question is asked, come forward promptly with your suggestion. It is surprising to see how soon leadership in more important things will naturally gravitate to the person who takes the lead in smaller things.

Lack of practice in making judgments. It may seem to a person who is in a minor executive position only, or possibly not yet an executive at all, that it will be extremely difficult for him to get practice in making judgments; but this is not at all true.

[1] From *The Art of Leadership,* Ordway Tead (McGraw-Hill Book Co.).

No matter what anyone's position may be, he may form a judgment on anything he wishes.

Of course, it may not be his right to take any action about the matter. But he can reach a decision as to what he would do if he were in charge, and he can check the accuracy of his own judgment by watching actual results and deciding what would have happened had his decision been put into effect. This check should be followed by an analysis of the reasons for any mistakes he may have made. There is no limit to the amount of practice anyone can, in this way, give himself in forming judgments even on important and complex matters. There is an advantage, other than just the practice it gives, in this habit. When someone does ask for an opinion, probably the question will have been considered quietly in advance, and a carefully considered answer can be given rather than a "snap judgment."

One chief executive, who has had much experience in developing and promoting junior executives, makes it a rule in his organization that no one, no matter how minor his position, may ask for information as to how a job is to be done without first stating his opinion as to how he believes it should be done. For example, a new clerk in the mailing department should say, "I believe it is all right to send this by parcel post, is it not?" rather than, "How shall I mail this package?"

This is a good practice for every supervisor to encourage in those under his supervision—also a good practice for him to follow himself.

Poorly managed personal finances. There are few things which will more completely take away a man's courage, and therefore his initiative, than to have his personal finances in such condition that there is a constant shadow of fear as to just what would be the consequences if he should make several incorrect decisions and lose his job. With a sensible person, a substantial savings account will not by any means make him careless as to whether or not he loses his job; but it will remove the cloud of fear and permit normal functioning of the mind. A well-planned personal budget plays an important part in success in supervision as well as in almost every other thing we do.

Developing constructive inventiveness. To a certain extent this important quality is inborn, but probably not to nearly so great an extent as we often think. It can be developed. If we study any example of the use of an original or ingenious method, we shall find that rarely is the thing we consider original entirely so. It is usually the ingenious application or adaptation of something one has seen or has used in some other type of experience. The person who noted how a large manufacturing shop controlled its stock of small parts so as to know just when it was necessary to start a new order through the process of manufacture might easily find in this the necessary material to use in the design of a new and ingenious system of stock control for the notions department of a retail store—and vice versa.

We should cultivate the habit of observing how people do things in all lines of work, and asking why. And usually those we ask are glad to tell us if we ask tactfully and show interest. People like to talk about themselves and their work.

4. *Tact*

Most successful men and women possess the ability to win the loyalty and support of those around them by saying and doing those things which give to others, especially to those under their supervision, a feeling that they are playing an important part in whatever is being done. The quality that enables them to do this we call *tact*.

Unfortunately, however, there are some men and women, apparently successful by all the usual standards of measurement, who seem to take delight in riding roughshod over the feelings of others, especially of those in lower positions who dare not show their resentment and who can only squirm and wish for the day when the tables are turned.

But I noticed one thing during the depression years. It was those men and women who had felt it wholly unnecessary even to try to be tactful who lost their jobs as executives in stores and shops and who came, meekly now, to the employment offices of other organizations *asking for anything that might be offered.*

Thus tact is not only helpful in the achievement of success, it serves also as an important insurance against loss when that which has been achieved is threatened by hard times and business retrenchment.

Dealing tactfully with the people under your supervision so as to cause them to like you as well as to respect you is so important to success in supervision that an entire chapter is given to a discussion of that subject (see Chapter IV).

5. *Enthusiasm*

Enthusiasm is defined as "an intense and eager interest in and devotion to a cause, a pursuit, or an ideal."

It is a state of mind that does not surrender readily to difficulties, but overcomes them. There are few other traits more universally possessed by successful supervisors than enthusiasm and the ability to arouse enthusiasm in others. Little can be accomplished in leading people without it; but the type of enthusiasm necessary is not the pep-and-go variety put on just for an occasion. It must be built on a firm foundation.

First, there must be genuine interest.

That should be easy, because there is no game or sport in which one may participate for sheer amusement which has more things in it to make it interesting than the business of supervising people. Supervision is intricate, and calls for the best thinking of which anyone is capable. It has variety; no two persons are just alike. It has in it an element of chance and excitement; the outcome of every decision is in the balance. And, finally, it offers a real reward for success.

Next, there must be knowledge.

No game can long remain interesting unless one endeavors to learn more and more about it. The supervisor who would develop real enthusiasm should endeavor constantly to learn more and more about every phase of his own business and about people.

Finally, there should be achievement.

With interest and knowledge will come confidence in one's own ability, and the joy of successful achievement. Genuine enthusiasm will follow as a natural result.

Sometimes supervisors, because of their dislike of the "pep-talk" type of enthusiasm, attempt to hide the natural enthusiasm they feel about their work. This is a mistake. Employees should be made to feel the same enthusiasm the leader feels. This, of course, should not be accomplished by the admonition "be enthusiastic," but by building up in the employee those things which have created genuine enthusiasm on the part of the leader: *first,* Interest, *second,* Knowledge, *third,* Achievement.

6. *Emotional Control*

Threading through all five of the other qualities important to success in supervision and, if properly developed, serving as an aid in the steady and consistent exercise of all is the sixth quality on our list, *emotional control.* All too often we climb steadily for months, even for years, toward the achievement of some cherished ambition and then spoil it all by some thoughtless word spoken in a moment of stress, by allowing some small failure to cause us temporarily to lose courage, by letting foolish pride or prejudice unduly influence an important decision, by permitting timidity to keep us from doing the things we know we should and can do.

But emotional control does not mean the elimination or even the complete curbing of our feelings. To control is "to exercise restraining or directing influence over anything." For any large measure of success we must have strong emotions, we must feel deeply. We may even have deep-rooted prejudices which we find it impossible to eliminate entirely.

The degree of emotional control is measured not by how strongly a person *feels* on any subject, nor even by the justice and soundness of his feelings, but by how he acts; by the extent to which his feelings are so restrained and directed that his actions are ruled by reason guiding his emotion; by the extent to which he prevents his personal likes and dislikes of people or his personal prejudices from influencing his decisions; by the extent to which he keeps worry of any kind from interfering with his work efficiency; by how calmly and with what good grace he takes well-intentioned criticism, even though not tactfully made; by how little he allows some unpleasant or embarrassing incident to "upset his nerves."

The effort, therefore, should not be to eliminate the emotions, *but to control and channel them rather than to let them control us; so to restrain and direct them that they never cause us to say or do anything unfair or untactful or which will in any other way tear down the structure of success in supervision that we are building.*

It is not easy to achieve full control of the emotions and it probably never can be done entirely; but to a large measure, success can be achieved by following the four simple rules that follow:

1. Recognize the importance of emotional control to *your* success and *your* happiness in every phase of living; and make a firm resolution to improve.

2. Start by forming the habit of waiting just a second or two before commenting on any subject. This may occasionally allow someone else to get credit for some bright suggestion of which you, too, had thought; but much more often it will keep you from saying something which, in just a second or two, you realize would have been better left unsaid. And for this practice to be effective in keeping you from blurting out thoughtless comments in places or at times that will seriously affect your success, it is well in *all* conversation with close friends and at home with your family, as well as in conferences and in talking with your chief and with your employees, to form the habit of asking quickly two questions before you speak: "Is what I am about to say my *considered* opinion?" and "What will be the effect; will what I am about to say accomplish any good purpose?"

Most of us would gain the reputation of being wiser if we said less.

3. When you find yourself getting irritated at *little* things, such as poor service in a store or discourtesy of another driver on the road, form the habit of *relaxing physically* and trying to look as if you were not angry or worried. Almost instantly you will cease to be angry—and may even laugh at yourself for letting such a little thing upset you. Try relaxing physically when worried by more serious things also. It will usually reduce the worry enough at least so you can think clearly and plan calmly to correct the condition that has caused the worry.

4. Form the habit of trying to look at your troubles in retrospect. An old man once remarked to his son that he had had

a great deal of trouble in his life, but that most of it had never happened. Most of the things which have worried each one of us most seriously have somehow or other worked themselves out and have not actually been so serious. When you find yourself continually worrying about anything, try to realize that this trouble will probably, like the others, turn out to be not so serious. Resolve to try to look at your present worries in retrospect.

As I look again at this list of qualities so important to success in the profession of supervising people—thoroughness, fairness, initiative, tact, enthusiasm, and emotional control—I am reminded of one of my favorite Bible stories, that of Naaman, the leper. Naaman was an important man with his master, the king of Syria; but he was a leper. Through a little captive girl from Israel, he had learned of Elisha, the prophet, and was told that this man might be able to heal his leprosy. So, with much pomp and ceremony, he went into Samaria expecting that the prophet would, of course, meet him with all the honor due his exalted position. But Elisha merely sent a messenger saying:

"Go and wash in Jordan seven times, and thy flesh shall come again to thee, and thou shalt be clean."

Naaman was angry. Were not the rivers of Damascus better than all the waters of Israel? So he turned and went away in a rage.

Fortunately, one of his servants had the good sense and courage to approach his master with this simple, but wise advice:

"My father, if the prophet had bid thee do some great thing, wouldest thou not have done it? how much rather then, when he saith to thee, Wash, and be clean?"

Naaman did wash in the Jordan and the story records that his leprosy was cured.

The six qualities on the list are not "some great thing" you are asked to do. All of them are the homely virtues which those of us who are a little older remember from our copybooks and our school readers.

But believe me when I say that thoughtful and persistent cultivation of these six simple, homely qualities, and not "some great thing," is the fundamental requirement for success in supervising people and in life generally.

Suggested Supplementary Reading on Qualities Important to Success as a Supervisor

The Executive, Samuel W. Reyburn.

The executive attributes which Mr. Reyburn believes most essential are:

1. Health
2. Integrity
3. Intelligence
4. Industry
5. Practical Experience
6. The Inquiring Mind
7. Judgment
8. Aptitude for Teaching
9. Enthusiasm
10. Capacity for following through
11. Ability to marshal and co-ordinate all one's knowledge and talents and courage to put one's decisions into action

The Art of Leadership, Ordway Tead.

The following qualities are discussed in considerable detail:

1. Physical and Nervous Energy (Chap. VI)
2. A Sense of Purpose and Direction (Chap. VI)
3. Enthusiasm (Chap. VI)
4. Friendliness and Affection (Chap. VI)
5. Integrity (Chap. VI)
6. Technical Mastery (Chap. VII)
7. Decisiveness (Chap. VII)
8. Intelligence (Chap. VII)
9. Teaching Skill (Chap. VIII)
10. Faith (Chap. XIV)

Personal Leadership in Industry, Craig and Charters.

Some of the executive's attributes discussed are:

1. Forcefulness (Chap. II)
2. Personal Interest in People (Chap. IV)
3. Kindliness Without Weakness (Chap. IX)
4. Self-Confidence (Chap. XVI)

The discussion of how to develop self-confidence will be found to be especially helpful.

How to Supervise People, Alfred M. Cooper.

Mr. Cooper has asked many groups of executives to vote as to the "qualifications which are indispensable if a man is to become a good supervisor," and finds that the following eight qualities are almost always in the lists selected: intelligence, integrity, forcefulness, fairness, loyalty, kindness, knowledge of work, and health.

CHAPTER III

Understanding Human Behavior

WHEN our son was about two years old he developed a great fondness for pulling electrical plugs from the outlets and putting them back in again so that he could see the lights go off and on. One day, however, he must have touched one of the prongs as he plugged in the light because he got quite a shock. It was not severe enough to do him any physical injury; but it did show him that plugging in lights had its unpleasant as well as its pleasant features.

For a time the memory of that shock was so strong that he let the plugs entirely alone; but, three or four days after his unpleasant experience, I saw him with a plug in his hand looking at an outlet. He would get almost to the point of plugging it in, then back away; then almost plug it in again, then back away again. The want to see the light go on and the want to avoid a repetition of the unpleasant experience alternated in their control of his actions several times; but, finally, he put the plug down and went about other and less hazardous business. The want to avoid a repetition of the shock had won out.

At first I was merely amused by this experience of our young son, but then the thought came to me that in this simple incident was a better explanation than I could possibly write of the whole basic law of human behavior; for human behavior, the thing some writers and lecturers would make so complex, is just that simple.

Of course, as we grow older our wants and fears grow more numerous and more complex. Instead of one want (to see the light) pulling in one direction and one fear (of an electrical shock) pulling in the opposite direction, there are many wants of varying strengths pulling in different directions and many fears also pulling in different directions. But, exactly as in the case of the little boy, anyone's final action in any situation will be decided by whether the sum of all the wants and fears which favor the action is stronger at that moment than is the sum of all the wants and fears opposing the action.

For example, each morning when the alarm rings and I must decide whether or not I shall get up and go to work, the situation is something about like this:

To Stay at Home

1. I was up late last night and I am very sleepy.
2. My vegetable garden needs working and that is really important.
3. There is a good game at the stadium this afternoon.
4. Bill Smith is on vacation and he beat me the last time we played golf. I would like to show him a thing or two.
5. It looks like rain, and if I get out in the rain my cold will get worse.

To Go to Work

1. I need the money for so many things.
2. I read an article last night about absenteeism hurting the defense effort.
3. The foreman complimented me yesterday on my fine record. I have a perfect attendance record for this year to date.
4. Last year I went to the ball game and the boss saw me there. He didn't say anything but I know what he must have thought.
5. I think there is going to be a promotion soon in our department. An unexcused absence might hurt my chances.

Result: I get up and go to work.

If we examine these or the causes of any other of our everyday decisions and actions we shall see that *at the beginning of each and serving as the cause of each there was a want for something, often several wants*. This will be found to be true of all voluntary human actions. Even fear, which is often the cause of decisions and actions, is just a want to avoid some unpleasant happening.

> It is a basic law of human behavior that all voluntary action springs from and has as its primary cause the desire of each person for certain things, tangible or intangible, the possession of which he believes will bring him satisfaction or happiness.

The person's want may be for comfort or safety, for the satisfaction that comes when he has pleased someone he respects and admires, for the pleasure brought by commendation and applause, or it may be merely the want to avoid something unpleasant, such as being without a job.

But, whatever the person's wants, these will be the primary motivating causes of his actions, not the will or the wish of anyone else.

It is important for anyone who aspires to success in any endeavor which requires the co-operation and help of other people to get the full significance of the fact that before there will be any voluntary action by any person there must be three conditions present:

1. The person must feel a want for something. No one will ever do anything at all unless he wants something.
2. The person must believe or at least hope that some definite thing which he can do will help toward the realization of the want.
3. Finally, this belief or hope must remain in the person's consciousness long enough for the appropriate action to take place.

One of the most interesting examples I have ever seen of an attempt to influence action by making sure, step by step, that there were present the three conditions necessary for action is this advertisement which appeared several years ago in the classified section of the Washington *Star*:

> PAYMENTS on your home are made easy by renting a room. Renting a room is made easy by an advertisement in the classified section of the Star. Call District 5800; open until 9:00 P.M.

The advertisement appeared in the days when a large part of the population of Washington was made up of government employees with steady jobs, but low salaries. Many of them were buying their homes on small monthly payments and the want to find some way to make these payments more easily was an ever-present one.

This want is mentioned tactfully and skillfully in the first part of the first sentence:

Payments on your home are made easy . . .

Then comes step two, without any break. The definite thing which the reader can do to help toward the satisfaction of his want is told, as is also how easy it is to do that thing.

. . . by renting a room. Renting a room is made easy by an advertisement in the classified section of the Star.

But, if the reader must wait until the next morning to place the advertisement and, even then, walk some blocks to the nearest office of the *Star*, it is possible that he will put off taking care of the matter for a few days—possibly forever. So the third condition necessary to assuring that the desired action will be carried out is taken care of. It is made as simple and as easy as is possible for the reader to place his advertisement *immediately*:

Call District 5800; open until 9:00 P.M.

But let us rewrite the advertisement, *putting first the want of the paper and of the writer of the advertisement*:

> THE EDITOR of the Star has asked that the number of classified advertisements in the paper be increased, and I am anxious to make my quota. Don't you have a room you would like to rent?
>
> The income would, undoubtedly, be of assistance in meeting the payments on your home. Our office is open every evening until 9:00 o'clock and the telephone number is District 5800.

The difference in appeal is so obvious that no comment is necessary.

As supervisors, we are most effective in capturing the interest and attention of those we supervise and securing desired action when we begin with a tactful reference to a want of the employee and then, and only then, show him how the doing of what we want will help him to get what he wants. What he wants should always retain the dominant position in our thinking, in our speaking, and in our whole technique of supervision.

People Want Only Five Things

1. *To feel more important, more worthy, more worth while*

Each person wants, probably more strongly than he wants any other one thing, to have and to hold a feeling of personal worthwhileness, self-respect, self-esteem; to be able to compare himself with his associates and not feel ashamed. This want is so strong and so broad in its application that it is probably the prime mover in more things that each one of us does than is any other single want—possibly more than all the other wants put together.

Glance through the advertisements in any newspaper or magazine and see how many of them appeal to this want; and see, too, how broad is the appeal, ranging from the advertisement, "Be the life of the party; astonish your friends with your ability to play the piano," to the dignified appeal to purchase a fine automobile, or even a handsome tombstone.

I once listened to a talk given to a group of business executives, meeting to study supervision, by a man who had been outstandingly successful in organizing volunteer groups doing various types of war work. His technique was simple. He tried constantly to find something that would honestly be praised in the work of each person assigned to any task. When any newspaper article was published, he was most careful to see that the other persons' names rather than his appeared in the headlines. When praised in public himself, he thanked the speaker politely, but said that he felt the real credit belonged to the chairman and members of the various committees.

This appeal to the desire for approval by their associates, which everyone feels so strongly, is often used most effectively by officers of clubs, Sunday schools, or other organizations where all the help they can get from other people is purely on a voluntary basis without the possibility of any financial reward.

Yet we all know presidents of clubs, indefatigable workers themselves, who complain frequently about lack of co-operation, saying that "everyone seems to expect me to do all of the work; and I might as well do it, because, if I don't, it will just not be done." Often such presidents are capable and sincere men and women, but they fail because they do not do the two things which are probably more important to success in leadership than any other things: to give credit frequently and publicly to all who help, and to refrain from making any public complaint, even when someone fails to keep a promise.

Skillfully and judiciously used, commendation can be made one of the strongest of incentives to better work in business organizations also. One large corporation, copying the military service, distributed mimeographed "citations" for unusual service. A letter or memorandum to a higher executive telling him of some valuable suggestion one of your employees has made serves the same purpose, assuming, of course, that a copy is given to the employee.

Contests with public announcement of the winners are good, if they are absolutely fair; but fairness is so difficult to achieve that, on the whole, contests are of doubtful value.

Probably the most nearly universal manifestation of the basic want for a feeling of greater importance is the desire of everyone to be remembered. Nothing pleases any person more than to enter an office and be greeted pleasantly, *by name*. Nothing can displease him much more than to come in several times, and each time find it necessary to introduce himself before stating the purpose of his call. Many important accounts have been won or lost for no other reason than because some employee remembered, or failed to remember, the customer's name. In Chapter IV there are definite suggestions on how to cultivate a good memory for names and faces.

Employees, too, like to be remembered. The department head who remembers that Tuesday will be the birthday of his assistant's little boy, and suggests that he leave an hour early or take an extra hour at noon so as to be home for the party, is building loyalty that will repay him many times for the trouble he has taken to remember.

One of the most sacred things in the life of every person is his *feeling of self-respect.* Even one in a minor position has a strong desire to maintain this feeling, and he resents deeply, even though it must usually be silently, the slightest suggestion of ridicule or any other evidence of a superior feeling on the part of his supervisor. *Sarcasm and ridicule have no place in intelligent supervision.*

The skillful supervisor tries to assign each job in a way that pleases, certainly never antagonizes. A person may often be won over by "This is an important and difficult job, but I believe *you* can do it" or "This is a difficult job; it is going to call for all that's in you to put it over, but I know you can do it." If the job is not sufficiently important to justify such a comment, just "Will you take care of this for me?" will have the same effect. In other words, the supervisor is paying the compliment of *asking* that the job be done, although he does have authority to *order* it done.

Mr. J. David Houser, whose job was finding out just how people feel on a wide variety of subjects, made this interesting comment: "Most dramatis personae of business usually prefer to do things in ways which are personally pleasing rather than to make money. No external influences—profit among them—are so strong as the urge for self-expression. Ego transcends profit."[1]

In addition to acting as a strong primary cause of action itself, the want for a feeling of importance or worth-whileness also exercises a powerful influence on just what suggestions concerning the other wants will be given any consideration at all by the person; and often it seems to exercise rather poor judgment in which suggestions it accepts and which it rejects.

The explanation is simple. We enjoy so much any experience in which the net total of all we think good or worth while about ourselves increases (expansion of the ego) that we tend to prolong that experience. On the other hand, we dislike so strongly any experience in which the net total of this feeling of worthwhileness decreases (deflation of the ego) that we try to bring the experience to a close just as promptly as we can. If we must remain in the company of the person or continue to read the letter or listen to the speech that caused the deflation, we build up an emotional wall, usually anger, which effectively keeps out any further suggestions from that source. And this applies to suggestions which are related entirely to other wants and would probably be accepted and acted upon were it not for the emotional wall or "insulation" with which we have surrounded ourselves.

Did you ever try to reason with a child after you had made

[1] From *What People Want from Business*, J. David Houser (McGraw-Hill Book Co.).

him angry? No matter how reasonable your suggestions were, no matter how pleasing to the child they would normally have been, the answer was "No!" It was as if every door to the child's reasonableness had been closed tight and your normally pleasing suggestions were not even heard.

Psychologically, this is exactly what did happen.

And there is not a great deal of difference between the child and the adult, except that the adult has learned to conceal his emotions more effectively than has the child. It is of major importance, then, that every contact with any person you would influence in any way at all should begin with something which pleases that person by making him feel at least a little more important. This is true whether the contact be through printed advertising, letter, public speech, or personal interview.

The first concern, therefore, of any person who would influence others should be to find a satisfactory answer to the question:

What can I say or do at the start which will make this person or this group feel more important, more worthy, more worth while, but which will not pull attention away from my major appeal?

And this is true even though the purpose of the interview is to correct some fault, some fault so serious that it is necessary to tell the person that unless he improves he will be discharged.

2. *To live safely, securely, and comfortably (Self-preservation)*

Self-preservation is often called the first instinct. All normal people want to continue to live, and if anyone can be convinced that a given action will make more certain that he will live, there is a strong probability that he will do that thing. Effective use of this want may be made in safety campaigns, in the sale of certain types of automobile equipment, or in guiding the choice of which of several means of transportation will be used.

For most of us, however, the fear that sudden death may be lurking around every corner does not exist, and efforts to influence us which attempt to appeal to the sheer desire to avoid death or dismemberment are not so effective as it would seem that they should be.

But there is another want, closely related to the instinct for self-preservation, which some observers have put as the most dominant in the minds of the great mass of working people. It is the *want for a feeling of assurance that their jobs will be permanent, that they will have an opportunity to work and earn on through the years.* There may have been times when this was not true; but in all except boom times this want for a feeling of security is one of the strongest wants to which any supervisor may tie his appeal to an employee to do a better job. But this should be done positively, not negatively. The supervisor may suggest that what he is asking to have done will give the person wider experience, more knowledge, more contacts, all of which will add to his value to the organization. Many ways may be found to tie to this want. It is not necessary, nor is it even advisable in most cases, to mention the want directly. The more subtle the appeal, the stronger it is; and this is true of the appeal to any want.

Also related to the drive for self-preservation is the *desire for personal comfort.* First immediate safety, then long-range security, then comfort. The advertisement which causes a man to picture himself leaning back comfortably in a chair, custom made and upholstered to fit his exact size and figure, may not be appealing to the most powerful want; but it is a strong one, especially in prosperous times. And having *comfortable* working conditions is often fully as important in promoting morale as having *safe* working conditions.

During World War II there was a demonstration of how a desire for continued comfort may have even more effect on our actions than fear of sudden death. For years effort had been made through telling people of the dangers of fast driving. Then came the announcement that when our present tires were gone it would be practically impossible to get new ones. Immediately we all began to drive more slowly, more carefully, and traffic accidents were reduced. We would not slow down to save our lives; but when it looked as if we must slow down or give up our automobiles and ride the streetcars and buses, we slowed down.

The appeal to one's desire for comfort, provided the connection between the desired action and achievement of comfort is definite and immediate, is a strong one.

3. *To find the right mate and to rear a family (Race Perpetuation)*

This, also, is a strong want. It may, at times, be even stronger in its influence than the desire to live, as most safety workers have found to be a fact. A picture of a mother and children waiting at home for the father, who, because he has been careless, will never come, has a stronger appeal even than the appeal to the man's own desire to live. Where an employee has a family, the skillful leader mentions it as often as possible. He asks about a child who has been sick or comments about a son or daughter who has won a prize in school, indicating that he remembers both that the person has a family and some of the details about the family. Nothing can be more effective in building loyalty.

4. *To explore the unknown; to satisfy curiosity*

We are all explorers at heart, and that has been true since infancy. Curiosity is one of the earliest of the instincts that influence the behavior of an infant, and its influence continues through life. While the supervisor does not have nearly so great an opportunity to use this want as does the advertiser, he can occasionally do so. The sales manager might say: "It's a new territory. No one has had it before. Frankly I don't know just what you will find; but I feel sure you will find it interesting and, knowing you as I do, I am sure, also, that if there is any business there you will get it" (appeal to curiosity and ego).

5. *Occasionally to escape serious reality, to be entertained, to play*

For the great majority of people, their work itself, if taken in a matter-of-fact, practical, realistic way, is somewhat humdrum. But everyone likes, at times, to escape the humdrum and have a little excitement. Many must satisfy this hunger by going to the movies, the ball game, or in some similar way rather than in their work. But the more the work can be given some of the elements of a game, if this is not carried too far, the better it is. Almost everyone likes to enter a competition, to play a game. That is why so many men like to speak of their work as a "game." All competitions for prizes and charts showing the relative standing of different departments appeal to this love of competition. Frequently the desire to win and be recognized as a winner is even greater than the desire for the actual cash reward. Contests thus often appeal to two wants, the first and the fifth in our list.

Appeal to as Many Wants as Possible

For an appeal to be effective in producing sustained effort, as many of the five basic wants as possible should be brought into play. A varied and well-balanced diet is as important in appealing to the psychological hungers as it is in appealing to physical hunger. The reason why religion has so strong and so broad an appeal is, probably, because it offers "food" to all the five wants:

1. *To feel more important, more worth while.* Jesus said these things to his disciples: "Follow me, and I will make you fishers of men." "When the Son of man shall sit in the throne of his glory, ye also shall sit upon twelve thrones." "Ye are the salt of the earth."

2. *To maintain one's own life.* The hope of everlasting life appeals to this want and also to the want for a feeling of greater importance.

3. *To find the right mate and rear a family.* The sanctity of marriage and the importance of rearing children properly is an important part of the teachings of most religions.

4. *To explore the unknown; to satisfy curiosity.* A desire to have a fuller understanding of the meaning and purpose of life and even a knowledge of what the future has in store is satisfied for many by a study of the Bible.

5. *To escape at times from unpleasant realities.* Contemplation on the belief that no matter how heavy the burdens here may be they will eventually all fade away offers an excellent escape and, if not carried to extremes, enables one to face problems and difficulties with renewed courage.

The reason why anything offering large financial reward has such an appeal is that, no matter what anyone's desires may be, the realization of practically all of them can be brought nearer by the possession of more money. In an appeal to the want for more money (true of all wants, but especially of this one) the supervisor should try to know and mention the specific reason why the person may want additional money—son just entering college, desire to pay off the mortgage, etc. This combines the want to be remembered with the want for more money with which the man may do more for his family.

Which Idea Will Win?

The problems of leadership would be simple if our suggestions and instructions had no competition; but such is not the case. Thoughts, suggestions, ideas are pouring in continuously from all sides, and any one of these may supplant the idea we have so carefully planted.

Let us take the simple example of the messenger sent to the file room for some papers the supervisor wishes to have promptly. The supervisor has issued his instructions, and explained that he is in a hurry. The messenger, anxious to please, runs down the steps rather than wait for an elevator; but on a desk in the file room is a magazine, a new magazine with the third chapter of a serial story the messenger has been reading. It will take only a moment or two to see whether or not the hero has escaped from the violent death that seemed to be his certain lot at the close of the second chapter. But no—the supervisor is in a hurry, and the desire to win commendation, combined with a realization of what may be the consequences of delay, is strong enough to keep control of his attention, and the magazine is not touched.

Ideas have varying strength in causing action. Some are weak, others so completely dominate the attention that they are difficult to resist. This relative strength is determined by three conditions:

1. The strength of the want or group of wants behind the idea.

2. The closeness and certainty of the connection between satisfaction of the want and the desired action.

3. The length of time the person continues to think about the fact that he can gain satisfaction of a want by carrying out the desired action.

These conditions point clearly to the four steps of the basic technique of influencing human behavior.

1. Review first the likes and dislikes of the person you would influence. Choose especially those wants, those ambitions which are powerful in his life.

2. Decide exactly how the attainment of one or more (as many as possible) of these wants can be brought closer by his doing

the thing you want done; and how best you can explain the connection, in a manner that will be definitely pleasing to the person.

3. When the proper opportunity comes, explain your proposition as effectively as you can, always keeping the other person's wants in the forefront of the explanation.

4. Find an opportunity, from time to time, to keep the idea fresh in the person's mind; but never overdo this.

The Part Played by the Emotions

We all know that anyone, even the janitor who sweeps our floors, can do his best work only when he is genuinely interested in what he is doing, when there is a feeling of confidence in his own ability to do a good job, and a sincere feeling of respect and even admiration for the person under whose supervision he works.

On the negative side, we know equally well how difficult it is for anyone to do good work when he is not interested in what he is doing, when there is hanging over him the feeling of fear that he may lose his job at any time, and, finally, when he so strongly dislikes the person for whom he works that there is a feeling of resentment of anything that person may say.

The only difference between the two situations is one of feeling or emotion—yet what a difference there is!

It is natural that there should be this difference, because emotion is really much more than just that "stirred-up feeling inside" which we consciously experience. The effect of a strong emotion is not something superficial, which can be brushed aside by the force of one's will; there is an actual physical change. The real function of emotion is to prepare the body physically for an action appropriate to that particular emotion. It does this through varying the normal secretions of certain glands. How complete the preparation is, is evidenced by the fact that anger—the emotion which, if allowed to express itself, would lead to physical combat and possibly wounds—causes a substance to be secreted into the blood which actually aids coagulation of the blood and thus decreases the probability of there being serious bleeding in case of a wound.

Other emotions call forth different secretions, each preparing the body for the action which that emotion would normally cause. Enthusiastic interest, for example, will cause secretions quickly usable by the blood stream in building energy and repairing any damage caused by physical effort. This explains why a person can work so much harder with no greater fatigue when his emotional reactions are in harmony with the task than he can when he is emotionally upset or when his feelings rebel.

The Imagination

Often, in our minds, we picture ourselves living through certain situations, and we feel all the emotions just as if the whole thing were real. The mental power that enables us to do this we call Imagination.

Imagination plays a much more important part in our lives than we sometimes think.

It has often been said that a man who never dreams never does anything great. The boy who works his way through college, giving up almost all pleasure and wearing shabby clothes, does so because his dream of someday being a great lawyer, doctor, or engineer has given to the idea of getting an education so great an emotional charge that the want for immediate pleasure makes little or no impression on his consciousness. The power of imagination to cause an appropriate action has long been recognized by advertisers of such articles as automobiles, motorboats, sporting goods, correspondence courses, and clothing. The automobile advertiser knows that if he can start you building "air castles" of yourself and your family gliding along over splendid roads up somewhere in the Great Smoky Mountains, far away from the city's heat and dust, sooner or later you will find a way to own a car. What really happens is that, through the use of imagination, the want has been given an emotional charge that makes it stronger in producing action than are wants with less emotional charge.

Purposeful thinking, even dreaming, on the part of the boy working his way through college, or even of the man skillfully guided by the advertiser to imagine himself driving his own car, should not, however, be confused with purposeless "daydreaming" with no effort to make the dreams come true. In this there are two serious dangers:

The first is the danger of the emotional charge thus aroused causing action wholly undesirable. Thus, the bank teller who dreams constantly about what he would do if he were wealthy, but does not lay his plans to become wealthy through the channel of hard work and judicious investment, may find himself endeavoring to realize his dreams through stock market gambling with money "borrowed" from the bank. The second danger lies in the fact that the logical result of any emotion is some action and, if we constantly allow our emotions to be keyed up to some high pitch through daydreams and then let the emotions die out without causing any action on our part, we are likely to find that our emotions will become incapable of causing action when we wish them to do so. It will be like pumping up a tire that has a leaky valve. In spite of these dangers, the imagination is a powerful mainspring of action, and we should learn how to use it as such, for our own health and advancement, and learn also how to make our appeal to the imaginations of those whom we would influence.

The imagination that counts is the one which combines reason with dreaming, which first checks everything calmly to see that the picture it has painted is really possible of attainment, then considers carefully what are the necessary steps, and, finally, takes these steps one at a time. Do not discourage dreams in yourself or others; but do direct the energy generated by these dreams into taking proper steps which will assure at least a fair measure of realization of the dreams.

The Will

What part, then, if any, does the will play in influencing decision and action? Older psychologists laid great stress on the importance of the will as a determining factor in human action. To train us to have strong will power, so as to resist the temptations that beset us on every side, was the ambition of our parents and our teachers. The will was often defined as something apart from the mind, a supervisor of our actions, a faculty that enabled us to decide between two or more courses of action.

The modern idea is that there is no such separate faculty. The question of which of two actions one will take depends on the relative "pull" or urge of the wants and ideas themselves.

Whether one stays in and studies or goes to the movies depends not so much on "force of will" as on whether or not the picture of future profit or pleasure to be gained from study is strong enough to keep out the picture of the more immediate pleasure of seeing one's favorite motion-picture hero.

This concept, that human decision and action are due rather to the relative strength of various pulls or incentives than to the arbitrary action of some faculty apart from the mind, has a most important bearing on every phase of dealing with people.

The Nervous System as the Organ of Learning

In order to understand how these pulls and resistances function, it is necessary to look at the nervous system.

Throughout our bodies, extending to the most remote parts, there is, as we know, a vast network of nerves that may be compared to an intricate electrical system. Just what a person does in response to any stimulus seems to depend on the connections established in this nervous system. It is much like the action of an automatic electric elevator. When you push the button on a certain floor, you give to the system the "stimulus" necessary to start a chain of events. The current is turned on so that the elevator motor starts. After a certain speed is attained, more and more power is applied until the elevator has attained its full speed. Then, just before the elevator reaches the desired floor, the current is cut off and the brake is applied. The car stops exactly at your floor, and the door is unlocked so that you can step in. Did you ever go upstairs to change your shoes or some minor article of clothing and, before you realized it, find yourself almost undressed and ready for bed? Just as the action of the elevator was due entirely to connections in the electrical system, so your action in unconsciously going ahead with your usual steps of getting ready for bed was due entirely to connections established in your nervous system.

By changing the connections the electrician can make it so that, when you press the same button, the elevator will do something entirely different. The connections in the nervous system, also, may be changed and new connections established. A person's final action, then, will be due to the resultant "pull" of a rather complex group of tendencies or incentives, which are in turn due to connections in the nervous system.

As a person goes through life, his everyday experiences are constantly forming new connections in his nervous system, and thus making new tendencies. A tendency to act in a certain way because of having acted that way before is spoken of as "learned behavior," or, more commonly, as *habit*.

The Law of Learning

There is one basic law of learning. It has been called, variously, "the law of learning," "the law of habit," "the law of memory." It is applicable to teaching, to the correction of bad habits in oneself or in others, to the development of memory, to advertising and selling, and to any other phase of influencing or changing human behavior, one's own or that of someone else.

It is so important that it should be memorized. It may be stated as follows:

> *The Law of Learning*
>
> Any connection, nervous or mental, that has once been made tends to recur.
>
> The strength of that tendency depends upon the INTENSITY, FREQUENCY, and RECENCY of the connection in past experience.

Intensity. We see and hear many things that make little or no impression on us, and they are forgotten almost instantly. Other things, because their first impressions were so intense, are remembered for years. A study of the factors that will increase the intensity of the first impression is well worth the attention of teacher, salesman, and supervisor.

Frequency. The more often any connection is made the stronger it becomes. Figuratively speaking, it is as if the pathway over which the nerve current travels had become more deeply worn. Many national advertisers use this factor almost exclusively, through use of often-repeated slogans. Every teacher, too, knows the value of repetition in establishing firmly what he has taught.

Recency. Other things being equal, that connection will recur which has been most recently made. The teacher knows that he must not allow too much time to elapse between the teaching and the doing, if he expects the teaching to be remembered. The advertising manager, too, knows how much pulling power an advertisement loses if the customer is prevented by rain or other cause from coming in the first day after the advertisement appeared.

Establishing Good Habits; Correcting Bad Habits

This brief heading really summarizes a large part of the work of supervision, the establishing of good work habits and the elimination of any that are bad—both in the supervisor himself and in those under his supervision.

William James, in his little book *Habit*,[2] gives an interesting explanation of the application of the "law of learning" to the forming of good habits. A summary of his rules follows:

1. When trying to eliminate a bad habit, always substitute a good habit, and concentrate on teaching the good. The bad will largely eliminate itself. The less it is talked about, the better. Resist not evil, but overcome evil with good.

2. Launch the new habit with as strong and decided an initiative as possible. This may be done by giving the reasons why it is important to form the new habit—how it will prevent error, greatly speed up work, bring rewards, etc.

3. Never permit even a small exception until the new habit is well established. It has been demonstrated that the very doing of the thing incorrectly, even once or twice, forms connections that will cause a tendency to fall back unconsciously into the incorrect way, even though the person knows better and does not intend to do it.

4. Practice the new habit promptly, and continue to practice it *frequently* until it is thoroughly established. The connection, even though firmly established by practice immediately after the instruction, will grow less and less definite unless it is renewed by frequent repetition.

[2] Henry Holt & Co.

We Are More Alike Than We Are Different

One of the most helpful things for the supervisor to remember as he endeavors to understand people is that, although as individuals we may differ in many ways from each other, we are really more alike than we are different. If, then, he would know what will be the reaction toward a certain change in the rules, let him put himself in the employee's place, forgetting for the moment his interests and his desires as a supervisor. If, as an employee, he knew only what he as supervisor is planning to tell his employees, would he, the employee, react favorably? Would he consider the new rule fair, considerate?

If the supervisor wonders whether or not he has been a little brusque in the issuing of instructions and has not told enough of the reasons why, he should ask himself—and endeavor to answer frankly and honestly—how enthusiastically he would work if the executive over him gave him instructions in the same manner. How would he react if his chief told him no more of his reasons for wanting things done a certain way than the supervisor tells those who work for him?

If you can develop this ability really to put yourself in the other person's place, without carrying over into your thinking your own prejudices, your own selfish interests; if you really can think as the other person would think, you have gone a long way toward a mastery of the real art of supervising people. For, after all is said and done, the simplest and best statement of the basic principle of personnel supervision was given almost two thousand years ago, in these words: "Whatsoever ye would that men should do to you, do ye even so to them."

Suggested Supplementary Reading on Understanding Human Behavior

Influencing Human Behavior, H. A. Overstreet.

Chapter II, The Appeal to Wants, is especially interesting.

Human Nature and Management, Ordway Tead.

The first ten chapters present one of the best available explanations of those parts of psychology which are of greatest interest to the supervisor. The style is simple and straightforward and when psychological terms are employed, they are adequately and simply defined.

How to Develop Your Personality, Sadie Myers Shellow.
The following chapters are especially interesting: IV. Habit Formation; V. What Happens Inside the Nervous System; VI. Breaking a Habit; XV. Emotions; XVI. Emotions—Inner Drives.

Handling Personality Adjustment in Industry, Robert N. McMurry.
An interesting discussion of the theory of personality is given in the "Manual to Train Interviewers," pp. 257–290.

New Techniques for Supervisors and Foremen, Albert Walton.
The following chapters discuss several aspects of the general subject of understanding human behavior: 3. Human Habits; 7. Personality; and 8. Resistance to Change.

The Psychology of Dealing with People, Wendell White.
This book discusses especially how to influence people by "appealing to the want for a feeling of personal worth."

Bodily Changes in Pain, Hunger, Rage, and Fear, W. B. Cannon.
A somewhat technical, but interesting discussion of this important subject.

Management and the Worker, Roethlisberger and Dickson.
This book tells in considerable detail the story of one of the most extensive studies ever made of how employees react to various changes in working conditions.

CHAPTER IV

Making Your Employees Like You as Well as Respect You

> "The deepest principle of human nature is the craving to be appreciated."—*William James*

It is important to your success as a supervisor that the people under your supervision should like you as well as respect you. We all work with more enthusiasm and less fatigue when we like the person under whom we work. The supervisor who would create in the people under him that somewhat intangible but most important something called morale, should give careful thought to those things which will cause people to like him.

The first requirement is fairness.

No amount of anything else he can do will cause his employees either to like or respect the supervisor who shows favoritism, who makes promises and does not keep them, who turns in careless or prejudiced ratings, or who, in any other way, shows unfairness. But assuming that every effort is being made to be absolutely fair, what next?

What Pleases People

There are two cafeterias near the building in which I work. On my first day here, I selected one, purely by chance, and on the second day I tried the other. There was not much difference, in either price or quality of food, so I bought a ticket in each and decided to alternate between the two.

But something happened to change this plan.

After about the third or fourth meal at the second cafeteria the girl behind the counter always remembered that I liked butter on my potatoes instead of gravy. The girl in the other cafeteria *never did remember this*, even though she had to throw away the potatoes several times.

Gradually I found myself going more and more frequently to the place where I was remembered, until, finally, I did not go to the first cafeteria more often than once or twice a month, and then only when I was with someone who wanted to go there.

That was a silly little thing on which to base a decision, wasn't it? *But you would prabably have done exactly the same thing, and so would about nine people out of ten.*

It would be difficult, indeed, to measure at all accurately just how large a part of why we like one person better than we like another, of why our business is given to one firm instead of another, is because just such little things as this have built up a feeling of good will toward the organization or the individual chosen; but the percentage is large—probably much larger than most of us would guess. And this applies to important decisions such as the selection of a doctor or deciding which supervisor we prefer to work for, as well as choosing the place in which to eat lunch or to buy a package of cigarettes.

Fortunately, the things that please people most are those simple acts of courtesy which are within the power of anyone to perform if he has a sincere desire to please and will give a reasonable amount of attention to the task. They are:

Greet each person promptly and pleasantly

There are few experiences more unpleasant to anyone than to enter an office or a room where there are other people and not be noticed or spoken to by anyone. Applicants or other business callers are willing to wait, if necessary, provided they are noticed promptly, greeted pleasantly, and asked to have a seat for a few moments.

Employees, even though you see them every day, like to be spoken to promptly when they come in each morning.

Be interested and show it

Whatever anyone takes the trouble to ask us about is important to him. It must be important to us, too, and we must show by our manner that we are interested and anxious to help in every way we can.

There is a tendency, after one has performed for a long time any task like giving information, interviewing applicants, or answering questions as to how to do a certain piece of work, for his manner to become mechanical. An executive talking to a group of branch office managers told of visiting an office where everyone worked in this mechanical, impersonal manner. He summed up in one sentence the visitor's feelings when he leaves such a place: "They were not discourteous, but they didn't seem to be much interested in me or my problems."

There is nothing more unpleasant to anyone than to have those to whom he goes for advice and help to seem not much interested in him or his problems. Be interested! *SHOW IT!*

Listen more than you talk

The surest way to win the reputation of being a most interesting conversationalist, one who is always welcome anywhere, is to form the habit of finding out what the other person is interested in and asking just enough questions to get him to talking about that thing. Strangely enough, even when a man has a proposition to "sell" or an argument to win, he usually is more successful when he allows the other person to do a large part of the talking than he is when he endeavors to dominate the conversation.

More than once an applicant has successfully "sold" himself to an executive just by listening attentively to that executive tell of his ideas on how a department should be run, only commenting briefly from time to time on how fully he agrees. (Don't let this happen to you—see Chapter VII.)

Say "Will you," rather than "You must"

Did you ever call on someone, possibly at his request and to do him a favor, and have some clerk tell you, "You'll have to wait, Mr. Brown is busy just now"? Didn't you feel like saying, "I don't 'have to' do anything of the kind; I'll just walk out"?

Such expressions as "you have to" or "you must" should seldom if ever be used even when you have the authority to do this. Even if "will you" fails to get the desired result—as, when, for example, an applicant continues to object to giving some information you are required to get from him to complete a form—some such statement as "I am sorry, but I am required to get that information before I can send in your application" is much less antagonizing than "you have to give us that information." There is a subtle distinction between "*I* am required" and "*You* are required," which makes the former much less antagonizing than the latter even though both you and I know that they mean exactly the same thing. I am the one who is taking the stigma of admitting that I must obey rules and orders instead of making you the one. And this simple, almost silly, little distinction means much more in pleasing people than it seems reasonable to believe it could mean.

Remember names and use them frequently

There is probably no one thing which pleases any person more than to be greeted *by name*. This especially is true of an applicant who has returned to see you a second time or a new employee whom you may have seen only once before.

If you find it difficult to remember names and faces, here is a simple and practical program which followed carefully and persistently will, in large measure, eliminate that difficulty:

1. *Get the name CLEARLY when it is first mentioned.* Too often a name is spoken rapidly and somewhat indistinctly, and we go ahead with the conversation thinking that we shall get it later. It never offends anyone if you say, "I always like to get a person's name correctly; do you mind repeating your name?" If the name is one which may be spelled in either of two ways, as "Green" or "Greene," spell it back, "G-R-E-E-N, or do you put an *e* on the end?" If you are at your desk, you can be casually writing the name down on a piece of paper as you spell it. If, later in the conversation, the name slips out of your memory, you can glance at the paper. Also, for many persons, writing a name and seeing it in writing impresses it on the memory more strongly than would repeating it several times.

If time permits, make some such comment as "I have a good friend, who came from down near Atlanta, named Sam Greene. Are you, by any chance, related to him?" This ties the name to a known name, and you can also be making mental comparisons between the two men in size, weight, appearance.

All of this seems like a rather long-drawn-out program which will take much more time than can be spared; but it usually takes only one or two minutes at most—no more than the useless exchange of remarks about the weather so often used as a "warm-up" conversation—and it is much more profitable to you and interesting to the person with whom you are talking.

2. *Repeat the name FREQUENTLY in the conversation.* One woman who has an unusual memory for names will, unconsciously, repeat the name as many as fifteen or twenty times in just four or five minutes of conversation: "Yes, Miss Jones, I think you are right" and, "Miss Jones, have you heard," etc. This habit is so strongly formed that she can hardly talk to anyone unless she knows that person's name, and so she usually asks the name of grocery boys, yardmen, salespeople in the department store, the painters working on the house, the janitor at the church; and she knows and uses all of their names. All of this takes practically no time at all, and is distinctly pleasing to everyone with whom she talks. This, like every other good thing, should, of course, not be overdone.

3. *Form an association between the name and some characteristic.* The next step is to find some way to "tie" the name to the person. This is usually done by forming some association between the two. You notice that Mr. Joiner wears a Masonic emblem; so, of course, he "joined" the Masonic lodge. I once met a man named Schnell and he talked very slowly; just the opposite of his name. "Schnell" is the German word for "quick."

We have two men named Sanders in the organization in which I work. One is in the appraisal division, the other is secretary of the Federal Intermediate Credit Bank. Their initials are E. P. and R. H. How can we remember the initials, and which initials belong to which man?

Let us follow the natural steps of establishing a connection. The appraiser's initials are E. P. What does an appraiser do? He estimates price. Estimated price—E. P.; that ties those initials to the appraiser.

Now, since Mr. R. H. Sanders, as secretary of the Federal Intermediate Credit Bank, does not travel so much as Mr. E. P. Sanders, we might easily say that his initials, R. H. stand for Right Here. These connections are somewhat farfetched, but they accomplish their purpose. I shall probably never forget or confuse those initials again.

Sometimes the connection is between name and personal appearance and, if so, that is excellent. Mr. Hardy is over six feet tall, powerfully built, deeply tanned, anything but frail, so the word "hardy" just seems to fit. Mr. Green is tall and I remember an old saying, "When you are green you are growing." With a little practice, some such connection between the name and what one does or what one looks like can be established for almost everyone. Even when it cannot, the study of the person and his name, made in an effort, even an unsuccessful effort, to establish a connection, helps to fix the name and characteristics.

4. *Use a systematic method of describing personal appearance.* It is surprising how little we remember, even about things we see every day, unless we consciously and systematically observe them. No better illustration of this can be found than to ask the average man to make a sketch of his watch dial. Try it yourself. Unless you are more keenly observant than nine out of ten persons, you will forget many things.

Many persons—detectives, for example—who must remember faces as a part of their work, have systems by which they mentally catalogue people. Almost instantly they observe, and impress on their memories, weight, height, coloring, forehead, eyes, nose, mouth, peculiar habits, etc.

One executive who visited the many plants of a large corporation on the average of only once each two years developed a code for his notebook by which he entered a brief description of each of the thirty or forty key persons in each plant. This practice accomplished three important things:

1. It developed systematic observation, so each important feature was seen and mentally photographed in the shortest possible time.
2. The writing down of the description strengthened the impression.
3. It also furnished a permanent record which he reviewed just before visiting each plant.

It is strongly recommended to anyone who has difficulty in remembering names and faces that, for a time at least, he adopt the practice of writing down, at the first opportunity, brief descriptions of those whom he meets.

When this practice of writing descriptions is first started, he will probably be surprised at the meagerness of the information remembered; but observation soon becomes systematic and almost unconscious, and a more adequate description can be written.

Thoughtfully, Conscientiously, Persistently. Success may not come overnight. Associations, carefully thought out, will become all confused. Attempts to "observe" so as to be able to write an accurate description will take the mind off the subject of the conversation. All of these things are discouraging; but time and time again this technique, when applied thoughtfully, conscientiously, and persistently, has overcome these difficulties, and has built real skill in remembering names and faces.

Stick to it.

One Simple Rule for Making and Keeping Friends

Perhaps all this can be summarized in one simple rule which should be applied constantly every day in contacts with people. It is:

> Always take every honest opportunity to say and do those things which make people feel bigger, better, more important.
>
> Never, unless it is absolutely necessary for their own good or unless circumstances allow no alternative, say or do those things, even in joke, which hurt people's feelings, which make them feel smaller, meaner, less important.

This does not mean that the supervisor who wishes to have his employees like him must spend his entire time making flattering comments to everyone in his department. To do this would probably have an effect quite opposite to that desired, because no one likes empty and insincere flattery. It is disgusting rather than pleasing.

But it does mean that you should consciously and consistently try to look for and comment pleasantly about things that are really worthy of favorable comment. A difficult piece of tabular typing done especially neatly and without error, the completion of a machine operation in better than standard time with a low spoilage record, a sales record that leads the department, are examples of things that offer such opportunities. Do not fail, also, to comment favorably on any improvement over past performance even though a high standard has not been reached. This is especially true in the case of new employees or those who have recently been corrected because of poor performance.

And favorable comments do not need to be confined to things that have happened in the shop or office. When you read in the paper or hear of some such event as a son or daughter of one of your employees winning honors, remember to congratulate the father or mother at the first opportunity. Even if the news item is just that the child has gone to some camp for the summer, mention it with some such comment as that you hope the child will have a fine time. Try to remember and use the child's name when you make any such comment. This adds more to the "ego-expanding" power of a comment than would seem possible.

One caution is offered because consequences of any failure to observe it are so serious. It is this: Be most careful to see that too large a share of the complimentary comments is not given to just two or three people in your department even though these people are outstandingly the best and really deserve all you say about them. Do not withhold deserved praise from these people, give them all to which they are entitled; but, also, find some pleasing things to say to the others in your department—all of them. There is no one whose work is so poor, no one even whose attitude is so poor, that there is not something that can honestly be commended. Take the trouble to find that something and you can discover, as many other supervisors have, that both quality of work and attitude will improve. There will then be more to be praised.

An interesting experiment demonstrating the effectiveness of praise in getting school children to do their best work was carried out by Dr. E. B. Hurlock of Teachers College, Columbia University, some years ago.[1] A number of children were first given a test to measure their ability at the beginning of the experiment. They were then divided into three groups, carefully selected so

[1] See *Journal of Educational Psychology*, Vol. XVI, p. 145.

that the groups were as nearly equal as possible in ability, in proportion of boys to girls, and in average age.

The next day they all assembled in one room for a second test; but, before the test was given, the children in Group I were asked to come to the front of the room. They were praised for the excellent work they had done on the preceding day and were encouraged to do even better, to try to avoid any careless errors, and to do as many problems as possible in the time permitted. The children of Group II were then called to the front and severely reproved for the careless mistakes and the generally poor work they had done. Members of Group III heard both praise and reproof, but no comment at all was made to them as to how they had done on the test. They were completely ignored throughout the experiment. The test was then given and papers collected.

This exact procedure was repeated for four days. The results are shown below:

	First Test	Second Test	Third Test	Fourth Test	Fifth Test	Per Cent Improvement
Praised Group	11.81	16.59	18.85	18.81	20.22	71
Reproved Group	11.85	16.59	14.30	13.26	14.19	20
Ignored Group	11.84	14.19	13.30	12.92	12.38	5

While, of course, the results of this one test are by no means conclusive, they do seem to point quite definitely to the fact that encouragement by the use of praise is the most effective method of getting people to do their best work. And this is borne out by the experience of practically every supervisor I have ever talked with who has taken the trouble to find the things people under his supervision do well and to praise them for these things.

And yet, how frequently most of us are guilty of that poorest of all techniques of supervision—saying nothing. We may assume, as did one supervisor I talked with recently, that the people under our supervision should realize that, so long as we do not find any fault with what they are doing, we are satisfied with their work. Or, perhaps, we take the attitude I have heard expressed many times, that people are paid for good work and good work is expected. Why, then, should the supervisor praise them when all they are doing is to give what they are paid for?

The answer is simple and practical. We should take the trouble to find the good things people do, to praise them for doing these things, and to offer help and instruction rather than reproof when we cannot praise, because to do this makes people happier in their work than does any other method of supervision. And it has been proved again and again that people who are happy in their work turn out a greater volume of work and work of better quality than do people who are not happy.

The One Personal Quality Most Important to Success in Pleasing and Influencing People

Some months ago I agreed to speak to a group of young business executives. As I was anxious to give this group something worth while, I read two or three of the best books I could find on the development of personality and prepared my talk most carefully. It was a rather elaborate speech, full of high-sounding psychological terms. I had worked hard in its preparation and I was proud of it.

But the speech was never used. Something happened on the morning of the day on which I was to give the talk that made me throw away all I had prepared, because it gave to me what is, I believe, the real answer to my question. And that answer, like almost all important truths, does not have any big words in it. Let me tell the story.

That morning I came into the office a few moments late and as I approached my secretary's desk she said, "I have a surprise for you this morning, Mr. Halsey, your royalty check is here." She was enthusiastic about the whole thing, being most happy to be the bearer of good news.

Now, there is one part of the story she did not know. Royalty checks come on time each six months so regularly that, if one were a day late, I should be sure that my calendar was wrong. Also, three months before this check came, there had been a letter from the publisher giving the exact amount due. I was expecting the check that morning, and its arrival, though of course welcome, was no surprise. *So my answer was just exactly what it should not have been:*

"Oh, that—I knew it was coming. I thought at first that you had a real surprise."

"Oh!" she replied; and I know she must have felt about like a toy balloon looks when you let the air out of it.

How much better it would have been if I had thought quickly enough to have said, "Isn't that fine. It surely comes in handy this month with two insurance premiums to pay."

I went on into my office thinking about the incident and worrying about it. It was one of those little things one does worry about because he knows that it would be made worse by apologizing. Suddenly the idea came to me that here was the answer to my problem. The quality most necessary for success in pleasing and influencing people is not something with a high-sounding psychological name—it is just this:

The willingness and the ability to control one's natural tendency to enhance his own ego by "showing off" just a little at every possible opportunity.

You might say that this does not apply to the incident I have just related. Surely I did not say that I knew about the royalty check with any conscious desire of "showing off."

Of course I did not! But there is that something in human nature which makes any person feel just a little more important when he knows anything, no matter how unimportant, some other person does not know. And it was this desire for a feeling of importance—a desire not consciously felt or identified as such by me it is true, but there nevertheless—that caused me to blurt out the remark I did.

It is replacing just such little, thoughtless remarks with remarks that definitely *make the other person feel more important* which is the largest single factor in pleasing and influencing people.

Let me illustrate: If someone tells a joke we have previously read, we would never assume a bored air and say:

"Humph! I read the Sunday *Times* too."

But I am afraid we might laugh and comment in about this manner:

"That is a good one isn't it—so true to life." And after a pause of a second or two, "It was in last Sunday's *Times*, wasn't it?"

I had an experience recently that probably illustrates even better how insidious is the temptation to indulge in this subtle form of bragging. I had been invited to speak at a meeting of teachers and on the way stopped at one of our state colleges to interview some of the seniors who had applied for positions in our organization. I had lunch with the registrar and one of the professors and on the way to the dining room I was jokingly berating the registrar about having snow every time I came to see him. There had been only a few flakes and the professor remarked that my speaking of snow reminded him of one winter he had spent in Illinois where they really do have snow, sometimes piled four or five feet deep, etc.

I could have said, "That's nothing at all. I lived for three winters in Wisconsin where they have snows that make the snows of Illinois look like nothing"—but I did not do that.

Quite unconsciously, I said something much more subtle—and much meaner: "I don't blame you for not paying much attention to my two or three little flakes of snow if you lived up there." If I had stopped with that all would have been well, but I did not. I continued: "I understand exactly how you feel, *because I lived in Wisconsin for three winters.*"

Not one winter but three; not in Illinois but in Wisconsin, where the snow is even deeper.

And to make the whole thing even more inexcusable, I did this when I was on my way to give a talk in which I had planned to tell the story of the royalty check and to discuss the principles it illustrates.

No, it is not an easy task to control the natural tendency each one of us has to say and do—usually quite unconsciously—little annoying things like this. But it is well worth whatever thought and effort it takes, because the quality which is probably more essential to success in pleasing and influencing people than any other is the willingness and the ability to exercise just that control.

Instinctively, we all dislike and avoid those persons who "make us feel cheap" by having previously heard all the jokes we attempt to tell; by telling about a man *ninety-seven* years old who milked *eight* cows every day when we have just finished telling, with considerable pride, about an uncle of ours who at the ripe old age of *ninety-six* milked *seven* cows every day. We all know how unpopular the habit of doing such thing makes a person and seldom, if ever, would we be guilty of doing them if we could only think about the effect before we do them. *But how can we do this?*

It has helped me in my own efforts to avoid doing these things to think of each situation where two or more people meet as offering just so much "ego food," just as if there were a table in the middle of the group with a basket of fruit or a box of candy on it. If any person grabs more than his share, someone must go without—and no one likes to do that.

Often, now, just as I am on the verge of blurting out some thoughtless remark, the picture of that table comes to my mind and I decide that I do not want to be an "ego-food hog." This simple little device has helped me so much that I feel sure it will help anyone who will try it.

Also, there is one important way in which "ego food" differs from ordinary food. If I restrain my desire for the larger piece of candy and take the smaller one, I do definitely have less food, and my hunger for candy is not so fully satisfied. But, if I restrain my natural tendency to show off a little and do not tell the "one better" which I know when someone else has told a story, there comes to me a feeling of satisfaction because I have exercised self-control and done an unselfish thing. And if I continue to do this, I experience the even greater satisfaction of having people like me, of seeing faces light up and the circle open when I join any group where I am known.

All this is "ego food"—much finer than I would have got had I grabbed more than my share in the first instance. It is as if I were being rewarded for restraining my natural tendency to grab the one large piece of cheap candy by being given a whole box of fine candy.

Saying "No" Tactfully

"Come on, driver, let's get the hell out of here. We are already a half hour late!"

We were on a through bus headed for Jacksonville, Florida, and had been running on time all afternoon; but, when we reached a junction point a few miles north of Savannah, the driver had announced that there would be a brief delay as a connecting bus had not yet arrived and our bus had to wait for it.

As we waited, one man kept complaining about the delay to everyone who would listen to him, and growing more irate all the while. Finally, when we were just twenty minutes late, he burst forth with his demand that we "get the hell out of here."

The driver could not go. He was required to wait for the connecting bus; so had no alternative but to refuse the request. What shall he say? It must be something that will both definitely refuse the request and placate the passenger; a difficult problem.

As an interesting test of your own tactfulness, decide *before you look at the driver's answer*, given later, just what you would suggest as the best solution and then see how it compares for both adequacy and tactfulness with the driver's answer.

His answer was, I believe, the most tactful I have ever heard used in any similar situation.

1. It was short—only six words. A person who is angry will not listen to any long explanation.

2. It expressed clearly the driver's desire to comply with the request, even though he could not. In other words, he did not make the mistake of putting himself at the opposite side of an argument.

3. It did not correct the mistake the passenger made as to how late we were. This would have made him still more angry and would have accomplished no good purpose.

4. It did not "chide" the passenger for his lack of consideration for the passengers on the connecting bus. This, too, would have only caused him to become even more angry.

5. It left two doors open—one for further discussion if the passenger really wanted more information as to why the bus could not go on, and the other for a graceful exit with dignity unimpaired (ego not lowered) if he did feel just a little ashamed of his outburst.

Here is the answer: "*I sure wish I could, mister.*"

And in those six words there is a better statement of the most important rule of how to refuse requests tactfully than I could write in six pages.

If, whenever it is necessary to refuse a request, we can always have a sincere, "sure-wish-I-could" feeling and *make that feeling evident to the person we are refusing*, we will have gone a long way toward mastering of the art of refusing requests tactfully.

Here are three simple rules which, when applied sincerely and conscientiously, will, in nine cases out of ten, successfully handle the difficult task of saying "No" without causing any feeling of antagonism toward the person who refuses the request or the organization he represents.

First, there should always be a sincere statement of regret:

"I surely wish I *could* admit you to the examination today—"

This feeling of regret can and should be present *and expressed* even though the request must be refused because of the person's failure to live up to previous agreements or to obvious requirements that must be satisfied before the request can be granted.

Second, unless the request is merely an angry outburst such as that of the irate passenger on the bus, there should be an adequate statement of the reason why the request cannot be granted. This may be brief, if the request is for some small thing, or in considerable detail, if something important is at stake. The example above might have continued:

> . . . but your application was postmarked December 2, and the rule, which I have no authority to change, states that, for admission to the examination given today, applications must be postmarked not later than midnight November 30.

Here the fault was obviously that of the applicant, because the time limit was printed in bold-face type on every announcement of the examination. But even when refusal is made necessary, as in this case, by the other person's neglect, there is no need to say, "*You failed to mail*," etc. Such statements merely antagonize without serving any useful purpose.

Third, there should, if possible, be a suggestion as to how the person may obtain at least a part of what he wants. The example given might continue:

> There will, however, be another examination on December 15, and, if you will sign this request, I shall be glad to have your application transferred. That will give you another week to practice your typing and so quite possibly get you even a higher grade than you could make if you took the examination today.

Try these three rules, applying them in the exact order given—regret, reason, suggestion—each time you find it necessary to refuse a request. If you are not already using this method you will be surprised and pleased at the result.

All the things discussed in this chapter are little things; some may even call them "pussyfooting." But, just such little things make the difference between tact and lack of tact; between causing your employees to like you or having them merely tolerate you; between success and failure on any job which involves meeting and influencing people—and how few jobs there are which do not require this!

Suggested Supplementary Reading on Making Your Employees Like You

How to Win Friends and Influence People, Dale Carnegie. Especially, Part II, Six Ways to Make People Like You.

CHAPTER V

Preparing the Job Specification

THE first requirement for success in selecting anything is to know exactly what is wanted. Selection of employees is no exception.

We usually blame our mistakes on the complexity of human nature and the difficulty of measuring human traits. I believe, however, that more than half of all the errors we make in personnel selection are due to the fact that, all too often, we neither know exactly what we want nor have made any definite plan for measuring the fitness of the applicant if we did know.

To express the same idea differently: I believe that, if we would carefully prepare a specification for each job and then use these specifications regularly and conscientiously, we could reduce our errors in personnel selection by not less than 50 per cent.

DEFINITION OF THE TERM JOB SPECIFICATION[1]

A job specification is a description of the duties of a given job or occupation and of the qualifications a person must possess to perform those duties satisfactorily. Suggestions as to the best methods of determining whether or not applicants have the desired qualifications should always be included. The information is usually given under the following headings:

1. *Identification of Job.* Symbol or number and title of the job;

[1] Since the term "job specification" is used more frequently in industry than the term "occupational specification," it will be used throughout this book; but both terms means exactly the same thing—"job" and "occupation" are considered as being practically synonymous.

The term "position" is used to designate a group of duties and responsibilities assigned to one person.

in which departments or shops it is found; job titles of closely related jobs which may be filled by use of the same specification; approximate number of people in the organization whose positions are covered by the specification.

2. *Description of Duties.* The description should make clear exactly what an employee in this job will be called upon to do and what are his responsibilities for the work of others. The description of the more important duties should be complete enough to show the reasons for the evaluation of the job given in section 3 and for the qualifications given in section 4 of the specification. Duties which are not especially significant in pointing out difficulty, responsibility, necessary qualifications, or unpleasant features of the job need only to be described briefly. It is especially important that hours of work be listed if these are different from regular hours.

The description of duties is usually prepared by a representative of the personnel division after an analysis of the statements of duties prepared by several employees in the job classification for which the specification is being prepared.

3. *Job Evaluation.* See Chapter VIII for a full discussion of this part of the job specification.

4. *Minimum Required and Desired Qualifications.* These qualifications should be stated in terms that are clear and easily understood by the layman and also mean specific and clearly defined traits or skills to the psychologist and test specialist. A psychologist with long experience in the design of pre-employment tests once told me that failure of practical employment men to state in understandable terms exactly what they wanted was one of the principal causes of the lack of success in the test programs in most business organizations.

Special requirements for individual examples of the job should be given. For example the specification might be for the job of messenger. Most messengers have no occasion to drive automobiles, but it may be absolutely essential that the messenger in the general office have a commercial driver's license because he must drive a small truck to the post office to take and get the mail. Many errors, serious errors, in selection are caused by overlooking these small but important requirements of special positions.

5. *Suggested Methods of Determining the Fitness of Appli-*

cants. See Chapters VI and VII for full discussion of this part of the specifications.

The Description of Duties

A statement of exactly what he does, carefully prepared by the employee and supplemented by explanatory comment and evaluation by the supervisor, is the starting point of many activities in personnel administration.

When this "duties statement" is to be used in the preparation of job specifications it should be so written as to serve three purposes, and all instructions to employees and supervisors should be prepared with these three purposes in mind. The three purposes are:

1. To give a general, but not necessarily detailed, description of all of the employee's duties. This should include duties performed only occasionally, if those duties are an essential part of the position. Sometimes a duty that is seldom performed but is definitely an essential part of the position may require a special skill and if it were omitted from the duties statement this omission might cause errors in selection and evaluation.

2. To give the personnel office all information needed for properly classifying the position as to both type (as clerk-stenographic, storekeeping, or production lathe operating) and *salary level* or *grade* (as junior clerk-stenographer, clerk-stenographer, senior clerk-stenographer). The factors taken into account in setting the salary level of the position are discussed in Chapter VIII.

3. To point out any especially unpleasant features of the position, such as unusual hours of work, standing all day, exposure to cold, dirty or dusty work, nerve strain, etc. Any especially pleasant or advantageous features, such as short hours, opportunity to learn a good trade or to live in a good climate, should also be described.

Typical Suggestions to Employees on How to Prepare a Duties Statement

The preparation of a clear and complete statement of all the duties of your position is made easier and a much better statement is usually obtained if the writing is done about as follows:

1. *Prepare a list of your duties.* As the first step, prepare a preliminary rough draft list, inventory style, of all your duties without any attempt to go into detail. Be sure that the list is *complete.* Include all the things you do both regularly and intermittently. Use a separate line for each separate duty or closely related group of duties.

2. *Describe each duty in sufficient detail.* The next step is to write a logical series of descriptive paragraphs covering each duty listed in your "inventory." No exact order of arrangement is prescribed, but it is well to include in the early part of the statement those of your duties which you consider the most important and those to which you devote the most of your time. Less important duties and those you perform only occasionally may come later. Indicate which is your regular work and which is done on temporary assignment, such as relief work when others are on vacation. Give enough of the details of what you do to provide a clear, definite picture of the difficulty and responsibility involved. It is, of course, not necessary to carry the details of the description to the extreme. Describe procedures only in so far as this is necessary to reveal the difficulty and complexity involved in your work. If you are required in your work to exercise considerable judgment rather than the mere following of established routines, so state and point out in just what part judgment is necessary. For example, if you are a stenographer, it is *not* sufficient for you to state, "I take dictation and transcribe my notes." What type of dictation do you take—regular office dictation, informal conferences, or formal hearings? What is the subject matter—routine correspondence, abstracts of title, legal briefs, etc.? What is the official position of those who dictate to you? Do you compose some or all of your own letters? How often? In what situations? Do you sign and release the letters you compose, or are they read by someone else before release? By whom? Do you do any other clerical or secretarial work? Just what? How much time do you devote thereto? To what extent does your supervisor rely upon your judgment? Is your work checked by someone else, or is it released without checking? Do you check the accuracy of the work of other employees? Is your check final?

If you are a supervisor, it will be well to indicate: (a) over what organization unit you have supervision; (b) what processes or functions you direct and control; (c) what part you have in formulating and developing methods, plans and programs; (d) upon what types of problems you make decisions that do not require higher approval and are not reviewed; (e) upon what matters you usually make recommendations rather than decisions; (f) to whom you are directly responsible.

Remember, too, that this is the one type of writing in which it is correct to use the pronoun "I" a great deal. *We are interested in knowing what you do personally*. To give us this information you must say "I write," "I assemble data," "I supervise," instead of saying that a certain thing "is done."

3. *Avoid as much as possible the use of indefinite words and expressions*. For example, such an indefinite expression as "I assist in" or "I handle correspondence in connection with—" does not give an accurate picture of exactly what you do unless followed by an explanation of "how" or "in what way" you "assist" in the undertaking or "handle" the correspondence. In the case of a typist assigned to the Statistical Division, for example, it is better to say "Do tabular typing from rough draft pencil copy of statistical reports, six to eight columns wide. Do final checking of own work and cut necessary stencils," rather than "Do general typing in Statistical Division."

4. *Indicate the degree of responsibility*. Your description of each duty should indicate clearly *the degree of responsibility you carry*. For example, if you make a report by obtaining required figures and information from several source records and assembling them in a prescribed form, it is well to indicate: (a) whether or not you are responsible for the accuracy of the transcript; (b) to whom you submit it when you have completed your work on it; (c) what verification, check, or review is made of your work and what approval is required; (d) if your own check is final and any subsequent review merely a general one.

5. *Indicate percentage of time*. In the margin at the left, indicate the approximate percentage of your total time you spend in the performance of each duty or closely related group of duties. Ordinarily it is difficult to do this accurately. Your best estimate will suffice.

6. *Most difficult duty*. After you have completed the descrip-

tion of your duties, add a paragraph indicating which of your duties you consider to be the most difficult.

7. *Most responsible duty.* Indicate also which of your duties you consider to be the most responsible as determined by such things as whether or not you are *finally* responsible for the accuracy and completeness and the possible seriousness of consequences if there should be an error in unchecked work. Give your reasons for considering it to be your most responsible duty.

8. *Supervisory responsibility.* Give a general statement as to the functions or operations you supervise and the job titles of the employees you supervise and the number in each job title.

9. *Unpleasant features.* Describe any features of the position which might be considered unpleasant by a new employee, such as irregular hours, standing for long hours, heat, dust, etc.

When you have completed this description of your duties, please give it to your supervisor.

Instructions to the Supervisor

1. *Accuracy and completeness of statement of duties.* Please read the statement of duties carefully and add any comments you may consider necessary, especially if in any case you do not believe the statement describes clearly enough exactly what the employee does or how difficult or responsible any duty is.

2. *Most difficult and most responsible duties.* Review the employee's statements on these subjects and give your opinion as to whether or not you believe the duties selected are the most difficult and most responsible. If you do not agree, please give your reasons.

Typical Job Specification

Position No. & Title	14–2—Clerk-Stenographer *85* Positions in the organization
Similar Positions	Secretary to Section Head
Positions Below and Above	Below: 14–1—Junior Clerk-Stenographer Above: 14–3—Senior Clerk-Stenographer

Description of Duties Under supervision does both clerical and stenographic work in which either the stenographic work is of more than ordinary difficulty such as: taking dictation which includes technical or highly varied matter or reporting meetings and conferences;

or

If the stenographic work is simpler in character, the clerical work is difficult and responsible in character including such tasks as assembling and briefing facts and information, preparing the more routine periodical statistical and accounting reports, indexing and classifying complicated material, giving out information on specialized subjects, composing correspondence involving a considerable variety of routine subject matter, or preparing legal forms and other papers without frequent instructions; or clerical work of approximately equal difficulty.

Hours Regular office hours; overtime infrequent

Evaluation[2]

Basic Training	10	Skills	8
Mental Alertness	10	Physical Effort	4
Responsibility N. S.	8	Working Conditions	00
Responsibilities Supervisory	0		
		Total	40

Assigned to Salary Range VII

Minimum and Desired Qualifications

Education: At least one year of satisfactory stenographic course. Prefer two-year college secretarial course.

Experience: At least one year of satisfactory stenographic and clerical experience. This may be waived if educational background and high test scores justify.

Skills: Typing at least 45 net words per minute, prefer 55. Shorthand, must pass 100 words per minute test, prefer 120. Ability to use calculating machines desirable in some positions.

[2] See Chap. VIII for explanation of the evaluation ratings.

Suggested Tests	Clerical Checking:	Minimum 60—prefer over 70
	General Mental Ability:	Minimum 40—desirable maximum depends on how much routine there is in position to be filled.
	Arithmetic:	Consider position to be filled—minimum of 80 if there is much work with figures.
	English Usage:	Consider position—minimum of 80 if letters or reports are to be composed.
	Typing:	Minimum 45—prefer 55 or higher.
	Shorthand:	Minimum 100—prefer 120.
	Interview:	If secretarial position, check especially—emotional stability and tact.

Suggested Supplementary Reading on the Job Specification

Manual of Job Evaluation, Benge, Burke, and Hay.
Contains an excellent discussion of how to prepare a job description.

Training and Reference Manual for Job Analysis, prepared by the Division of Occupational Analysis, U.S. Employment Service.
This manual contains probably the most complete and detailed set of instructions available on how to prepare a job description and make a job analysis. Copies may be obtained from the Superintendent of Documents, U.S. Government Printing Office, Washington 25, D. C. Price 25 cents.

CHAPTER VI

The Use of Tests as an Aid in Selecting Employees

Two complaints against the use of tests in the selection of employees are frequently heard:

First, that they are not fair; that some persons, no matter how skilled they are, or how much they know about the subject, become so nervous that they cannot pass.

Second, that tests do not give a true prediction of behavior on the job; that often a person who passes the tests in the employment office with high scores fails to make good on the job.

Both of these complaints are often justified.

Everyone who has administered tests knows that there are some people who cannot do their best if they know they are taking a test. But the question is, Is there any other method of measuring certain skills and aptitudes which will be *less unfair to the applicant* than the use of tests? If there were ten applicants for a position as typist, or cashier-wrapper in a store, or assembler of a small electrical device, is there any method better and fairer than the use of well-selected tests to enable the employment interviewer to choose the one person most likely to make good on the job? If all ten could be put on the job for a period of two or three weeks and their actual performance observed, that would probably be a more accurate method; but this would, of course, be much too expensive and would also be impracticable in other ways. Actual experience has, I believe, proved that well-chosen tests skillfully and sympathetically administered and interpreted are a great aid in achieving fairness in selection.

The use of tests is occasionally unfair, yes; but in the determination of certain skills and aptitudes it is less frequently inaccurate and therefore less frequently unfair than any other method I know.

While the question of fairness to the applicant is under consideration, it should be brought out that it is quite as unfair to an applicant to hire him for a job for which he does not have the necessary qualifications as it is to fail to hire him when he does have the qualifications. The goal of the employment selector should be to place people in jobs where they can be successful and happy. The person he does not select for one job may, in a few days, be selected for another one better suited to his abilities. The goal should always be to select, out of the group available, the person whose capacities and interests match most closely the requirements and opportunities of the job. If this is done skillfully and the new employee is properly aided in any necessary adjustment to new conditions, many of the real causes of labor unrest and grievance will be eliminated, and actual efficiency in production will be increased.

There is a growing recognition of the importance of happiness on the job. This will be discussed in detail in Chapter XXIII, but this definition is of interest at this point in our discussion:

"If I were to define real happiness or success on one's job, I should define it as the use of every single characteristic a person possesses."[1]

Perhaps the best answer to the complaint that tests do not give a true prediction of behavior on the job is to admit frankly that it is true. Even the best tests skillfully administered tell only what a person *can do* and not what he *will do* when he gets on the job. For example, a girl with an excellent score in finger dexterity and a somewhat better than average score in mental alertness would seem to have the necessary qualifications for learning to operate a loom in a cotton mill or to be a wrapper in a department store. She might, however, be lazy, or hard to get along with, or even dishonest, and fail for one of these reasons. She probably *can* make good; but whether she does or does not depends not only on the abilities measured by the tests, but on other qualities also.

[1] Dr. Johnson O'Connor, in the American Management Association's Office Management Series #79. Dr. O'Connor is head of the Human Engineering Laboratory and has had many years of successful experience in vocational guidance.

But if her score is low in finger dexterity it is reasonably certain that she cannot make good on the job even if she is industrious, pleasant, and honest.

The best use of tests, then, is to weed out those who cannot do the work. The final selection from the group who can do the work is usually best made on the basis of personal interview and investigation of school and work records.

Low scores in tests are more significant in predicting failure on the job than are high scores in predicting success.

The following section discusses the qualities and significance of tests and briefly describes some tests frequently used in employment offices.

What Is a "Good" Test?

In determining whether a test is suitable for use, several qualities should be considered. The most important is *validity*, or the degree of accuracy with which the test measures what it is supposed to measure. In the field of employee selection the validity of a test is the closeness with which test scores agree with some measure of actual performance on the job. This measure is called a *criterion.*

The degree of validity of any test—that is, *how accurate* it is as a predictor—is usually stated in terms of its *correlation* with the criterion. The *correlation* between any two variables, such as the scores on a test and a criterion, is their tendency to vary together. For example: assume the supervisor's ratings are used as the criterion. If all persons rated by the supervisor as excellent on a certain type of work make high scores on a certain test, if those rated as average make average scores, and if those rated as unsatisfactory make low scores, there would be virtually a *perfect correlation* between test scores and the criterion. Such a correlation is, of course, practically impossible, because, as explained earlier in this chapter, even a perfect test measures only the *ability* to do the work, and factors other than ability enter into success.

It is important also that any method of selection be *reliable.* A test is reliable if it can be depended upon to give approximately the same results each time it is administered. Many tests have alternate forms. The reliability of these is the extent to which the two or more forms yield the same results when administered to the same persons under the same circumstances.

Another important consideration is *face validity*, or the *apparent* relationship between the test and the skills or other qualities it is designed to measure.

The applicant who is refused a job because he made a low score in a typing test, or in making calculations of a kind he must make on the job, or in answering questions about some machine tool he claims to know how to operate is likely to accept the decision with much better grace than he would if his rejection were based on the results of a test in which he put dots in small circles or one in which he was asked to tell what came into his mind when he looked at each of a series of ink blots.

This does not mean that we should throw out all tests that do not have face validity as well as validity in fact. There are some qualities for which it is extremely difficult, if not impossible, to construct satisfactory tests with face validity. But whenever it is practicable to do so, tests which have this important advantage should be chosen.

The Meaning of Test Scores

When a test is first constructed, the author decides upon some method of scoring, such as five points for each correct answer. When the test is administered, the points are added up to obtain what is called the *raw score*. The raw scores of different tests are seldom directly comparable. Thus a raw score of 50 may be the average achieved in one test and a raw score of 175 the average achieved in another test.

The manuals which come with almost all published tests contain conversion tables so that the raw scores may be converted into other scores which are comparable, the most widely used being *percentile scores*. A percentile score is a numerical score which indicates what percentage of all scores made by a given class or group of individuals is lower than the individual's score. Thus a percentile score of 65 means that 65 per cent of all members of the group with which the person is being compared made scores lower than (or at most equal to) that person's score. A percentile score of 50 means that one half of the group made as low or lower scores than the individual and half of the group as high or higher scores.

The Meaning and Significance of "General Intelligence"

Intelligence is usually defined as the ability to learn from experience. As used in the vocational field, it is the mental ability to learn quickly the things one must know in order to perform satisfactorily the duties of a new job. There are many tests designed to measure this quality, which is variously called general intelligence, mental alertness, problem-solving ability, learning ability, and adaptability.

Studies have been made and tables prepared listing scores which indicate suitable mental levels for various occupations. In some of these tables, the term "acceptable range" is used rather than "minimum acceptable score," because experience has shown that, for practically all types of work, if there is intelligence enough to learn the duties of the position within a reasonable time, additional increments of intelligence are of little if any value in vocational success.

Persons making less than the lower score of the range should not be employed because they will find the work too difficult mentally. Those placing above the upper score should not be employed for the job in question unless it is believed that within a reasonable time there will be an opportunity for promotion to work of a higher intellectual level.

Scores much higher than the upper level of the acceptable range for any job predict three things only: (1) probability that the person will learn the work more quickly than the average; (2) probability that he may be good promotional material; and (3) probability that he will become bored and dissatisfied unless promotion comes reasonably soon.

Of course, there will be cases where, because of lack of ambition or courage, a person of high intellectual level is content to take the easy and safe course of doing a routine job so well that he is assured of a permanent position. This attitude can be determined best by interview.

Tests of Aptitude and Proficiency in Office Occupations

It is in selecting employees for office occupations that tests find their best application. The persons examined are accustomed to writing and, for the most part, accustomed to taking tests. And the tests can more easily be made actual "samples of the job" than in other occupations.

It is not surprising, then, that properly selected and interpreted tests show higher validities when compared with success on the job in simpler office occupations than in any other field.

One of the most widely used tests of aptitude for performance of simple clerical work is the *Minnesota Clerical Test.* It has been used for many years, and its validity in measuring the one thing it is designed to measure is probably higher than that of any other test in common use.

There are many good tests of proficiency in stenography, typing, and other office skills.

Tests of Aptitude and Proficiency in Mechanical Trades

Aptitude for the mechanical trades seems to be made up of several qualities.

Mechanical comprehension is the ability to perceive and understand the relationship of physical forces and mechanical elements in practical situations. Bennett's *Test of Mechanical Comprehension* shows pictures and asks questions. For example, pictures of two rooms are shown, one practically bare of furniture and the other with furniture, rugs, and draperies. The question asked is, "Which room has more echo?" Some of the other questions are much more difficult.

Manipulative skills, involving finger and hand dexterity, visual acuity, and muscular control, are essential in most trades. The *MacQuarrie Test for Mechanical Ability*, which measures these skills, has been used since 1925 and administered to more than five million persons. It consists of a number of paper-and-pencil exercises.

Skill in the use of tools is essential in most trades. Several tests have been constructed which measure this skill as applied to the different trades.

Tests of Personality and Temperament

The tests most frequently used to measure personality and temperament are of two distinct types:

1. *The Personality Inventory* is usually a list of from 125 to as many as 500 questions similar to the following:

Do you often worry about possible future misfortunes?
Do you tend to resent criticism even when this is justified?

The answers to significant questions are given weights according to the degree to which they indicate certain traits.

2. *The Projective Technique* for measuring personality and temperament is a relatively new development. The examinee is shown rather vaguely outlined pictures or ink blots and asked to tell what he sees, sometimes even to make up stories about what he sees.

Tests of personality or temperament of either type should not be used except under the supervision of a competent psychologist. Even then their predictive value in selecting employees is questioned by many.

Suggested Supplementary Reading on the Use of Tests in Selection

Aptitudes and Aptitude Testing, Walter V. Bingham.

List of Contents

Part I: Aptitudes and Guidance

I. Introduction; II. Theory of Aptitude: Basic Concepts; III. Theory of Aptitude, Concluded: How People Differ; IV. Intelligence and Aptitude; Nature of Intelligence and Ways of Measuring it; V. Intelligence and Aptitude, Concluded: Occupational Requirements; VI. Interests and Aptitudes: Nature of Interests—How They Are Ascertained; VII. Interest Inventories: Their Use in Counseling; VIII. Achievement Tests as Indicators of Aptitude.

Part II: Orientation Within the World of Work

IX. The World of Work; X. Aptitudes for Manual Occupations: 1. Heavy Labor— 2. Bench Work; XI. Aptitudes for Skilled Trades; XII. The Field of Clerical Occupations; XIII. Clerical Aptitudes and Their Measurement; XIV. Aptitudes for the Professions: 1. Introduction— 2. Engineering— 3. Law— 4. Medicine, Surgery and Dentistry; XV. Aptitudes for the Professions, Concluded: 1. Nursing— 2. Teaching— 3. Music and Art.

PART III. THE PRACTICE OF TESTING

XVI. Selection of Tests; XVII. Administration of Tests; XVIII. Giving Group Tests; XIX. Interpreting Test Performance.

Appendix: Description of Representative Tests and Interest Schedules.

Selecting and Inducting Employees, George D. Halsey.

A list of the titles of the chapters on tests follows: Introducing and Developing a Testing Program; Selection and Validation of Tests; Tests of Mental Abilities; Tests of Manual Dexterity; Tests of Aptitude and Proficiency in Mechanical Trades; Tests of Aptitude and Proficiency in Office Occupations; Tests of Personality and Temperament; Measurement of Interests; General Diagnostic Tests; Special Purpose Tests; "Home-Made" Tests.

Principles of Personnel Testing, C. H. Lawshe.

Each step of the process of installing a program of personnel testing is discussed. Several of the better known tests are described.

CHAPTER VII

Some Suggestions on Interviewing Applicants

THE interview has been defined as a "conversation with a purpose."[1] The purpose of the supervisor's interview with each applicant for a position should be twofold: (1) to find out how well qualified the applicant is for the position in question; (2) to make a friend for the organization.

Some employment interviewers seem to forget entirely this second part. They are keenly alert to everything that will give them a clue as to the applicant's abilities or, more especially, to any weakness or lack of ability which may exist. They even set "traps" to get the applicant to say or do things he would not normally say or do. But they ignore entirely the effect of all this on the attitude of the person being interviewed.

I remember once in my earlier days in employment work I hit upon what I believed to be an excellent plan for determining whether or not applicants for the position of section manager in a department store had the necessary patience and tact to handle properly questions and complaints from customers. I deliberately found some way to upset the applicant. I would lead him into making some slighting remarks about the state in which I was born and then let him know, none too pleasantly, that it was my native state. I would occasionally even imply that there was some doubt in my mind as to the truthfulness of some of his claims.

All this was reasonably effective in accomplishing one purpose, that of detecting certain traits that would be a handicap on the job. I always tried to explain, at the close of the interview, that nothing personal was intended, that it was merely part of the interview; but in spite of this, complaints soon began to come to the

[1] From *How to Interview*, Bingham and Moore (Harper & Brothers).

management about discourteous treatment in the employment office, and I quickly realized that good will of the public toward our organization was probably quite as important as avoiding an occasional error in the selection of section managers.

Of course, it must be recognized in any attempt to get facts about the personality of an applicant that there is often a lack of correspondence between behavior of individuals in what might be called "stress situations" and that observed when easygoing conditions exist. In interviewing for positions in which serious "stress situations" do frequently arise, such as that of police officer or army officer, a special interview technique has been devised.[2]

For the type of interviewing most of us will do, however, we shall probably learn much more about the applicant, even about how he behaves under mild stress, if we endeavor to keep the interview on a friendly informal basis and do not attempt to introduce any artificial condition of stress. Certainly we will be much more successful in the second part of our objective, that of making a friend for the organization.

Fourteen Suggestions for Making the Interview More Effective

1. *Decide carefully in advance just what you wish to determine and can determine by the interview*

For each position there are essential qualities which can best be determined by a personal interview. There are other qualities which are measurable by simple, standardized tests and these should be measured in that way. It would be foolish, for example, to depend upon an interview to determine accurately an applicant's speed and accuracy in typing or in performing simple calculations.

It is, of course, equally impossible to determine by means of talking to a person whether or not he actually possesses a certain mechanical skill; but there are questions carefully prepared for a large number of trades, which may be used to check with reason-

[2] For full explanation of this technique as used in connection with tests given police officers see "The Stress Interview," Freeman, Manson, Katzoff and Pathman, in the *Journal of Abnormal and Social Psychology*, October, 1942.

able accuracy an applicant's claim to be a skilled worker in those trades. The use of these trade-test questions is discussed in more detail in suggestion number 7.

2. *Examine and discount your own prejudices*

"The extent to which we are all more or less committed in advance to certain ungrounded convictions, opinions, points of view, or preconceptions is seldom fully realized. Everyone has some prejudices, whether he is aware of them or not. The open mind which is indispensable to successful fact finding is seldom achieved without conscious effort directed toward the discovery and elimination of the particular preconceptions and stereotypes of thought which obscure or distort the truth as it emerges during the interview."[3]

3. *Give personal appearance its proper weight; but no more*

Personal appearance, as noted by casual observation, is usually given more weight in the selection of people than it should be. This is true even in positions in production departments where there is no contact with the public.

In positions where the person is in frequent contact with the public, such as a salesperson in a retail store, smartness and attractiveness are definite assets; but it should always be remembered that personal appearance is only one part of the whole personality of the salesperson, and probably not the most important part.

I once asked a friend who was personnel director of another store to walk with me through the store in which I was personnel director and point out the salespeople he would have rejected on the basis of appearance had they applied to him. We then went back to the office and checked the sales record of this group. To our surprise it was only slightly lower than the average for the other salespeople. And in the group he had included our best saleswoman in millinery, and in misses dresses, and also one of our best demonstrators in toilet goods. In all three cases, however, these women had other traits which much more than offset personal appearance. All three were outstanding in the interest they always showed in the customer's problems and in their memory of names and faces and personal tastes of customers.

[3] From *How to Interview*, Bingham and Moore (Harper & Brothers).

4. Open the interview by conversing briefly and informally about some subject of mutual interest

Most applicants are nervous at the beginning of an interview. The first task of the interviewer is to put them at their ease, get them to "loosen up" so that they will answer questions naturally and without restraint.

One of the best openings is to ask about some mutual friend as: "Is Bill Sparks still foreman of the lathe department? How is he getting along?"

A question about the person's name is good: "I knew a Sam Greene from the same part of the state you come from, I wonder if, by any chance, he is a relative of yours?" This serves the dual purpose of acting as a "warm-up" conversation and helping you to remember the applicant's name.

The weather is not so interesting an opening subject as something more personal and individual, but it does have the advantage of being so completely impersonal that you can use the same opening for each applicant and thus avoid the possibility of treating one applicant more favorably than another.

5. Endeavor to talk to the applicant alone

If another person is with the applicant, or even in the same room and in easy hearing distance, it is practically impossible to have a satisfactory interview.

Frequently someone recommending another person will wish to remain. Some tactful way to avoid this should be found. One way is to say that you wish to give the applicant a brief oral test and you find people work better when no one else is around.

6. Ask questions which call for narrative statements—things done which have demonstrated the possession of certain qualities—rather than questions calling for an expression of opinions or a mere chronological statement of experience.

The chronological statement of experience is essential, with the entire time fully accounted for; but this should be given on an application form or in a letter, rather than in the interview.

It is well to decide in advance of the interview just what type of question will be understood by the applicant and will bring out the significant evidence.

For example, let us assume that the position for which you are interviewing is that of secretary to the head of a large department. Because of the importance of the position it has been decided that, to be considered, an applicant must have had at least two years of secretarial experience, and must be able to type at a speed of not less than 60 net words a minute and take dictation of unfamiliar material at 120 words a minute. The application and some simple tests will check these qualifications and weed out those who do not measure up to these preliminary standards.

But it has been decided also that *tact* is an important qualification, and that whether or not the applicant possesses this quality is to be determined by interview. Obviously, asking the question, "Are you tactful?" would not bring out much valid evidence.

But the following question might be used: "As you know, one of the most important duties of a secretary to a high executive is to get other executives in the business to do certain things the way she knows her chief wants them done; but she must often do this without asking her chief to issue orders. Have you ever had any cases where the other executives were a little slow about doing things or sent in some report which you knew would not give your chief the information he wanted?" Almost every secretary who has had the type of experience we want will answer that she has had just such problems to solve. The next question would, naturally, be "Just how did you go about correcting that condition?"

Sometimes when using this method of interviewing with applicants who have had but little business experience it is necessary for the interviewer to help the applicant by some such question as "Were you ever in a situation about like this——?" The situation should be one the successful solution of which would call for the qualities being measured and yet be within the applicant's field of experience—possibly in high school or college life for the inexperienced applicant.

"It is not necessary that every example of past demonstration of capacity be vastly important. Rather the candidates should be impressed at the outset with the fact that minor or unimportant episodes which demonstrate possession of the capacity are significant in proof. As evidence of demonstration of the possession of ingenuity, it may be as significant under the circumstances to have persuaded a taxi driver to lend you a dollar to buy gasoline, as to have persuaded the President of the United States to issue a proclamation. The significance will depend upon the circumstances. Facts, not news value, constitute evidence of personal capacity.

"One objection to oral examinations has been that they adduce evidence of affirmative possession of qualifications primarily, and that they do not adduce reliable evidence of negative characteristics. The process here described when followed through, results in lack of evidence of the possession of required qualifications when those qualifications are not possessed or have not been demonstrated in experience.

"But the process goes even farther in revealing lack of qualifications than the mere absence of affirmative evidence. For example, in the examination for Personnel Director the first factor to be evidenced was the possession of initiative, and the candidates were asked to give *examples* of the display of initiative in their past experience. They were encouraged to present profuse examples of ideas, plans, and procedures which they had initiated in order to evidence fully the extent of their initiative. A subsequent factor was the capacity to carry through a program to successful conclusion. Here the examiners were able to refer again and again to many ideas, plans, and procedures which the candidates had stated they initiated, and to ascertain whether they had carried them into effect or had simply thought them up and then allowed them to lapse. Where any example of initiative had not been carried through, the reasons and circumstances for the failure to carry through were placed upon the record, and this introduced the candidate to further questions of qualification such as ability to obtain cooperation and to adapt programs to changing conditions, and so on. Having made original assertions of considerable capacity for initiative, verified as to time, place, and details, the door was wide open for disclosure of lack of capacity to carry through which may have been due to lack of will, or lack of caring, or lack of daring, or fear of consequences, or—in some cases —to conditions entirely beyond the control of the applicant. The evidence was spread upon the record of the lack of capacity of the candidate as well as his capacity in respect to the several demonstrable factors."[4]

[4] From *An Approach to More Objective Oral Tests,* Ordway and O'Brien (Society for Personnel Administration, Washington).

7. Develop and use informally trade-test questions for the occupations under your supervision

While, of course, actual skill in any occupation cannot be measured directly by talking with a person, it has been demonstrated by many tests that there are for each occupation a number of practical facts, especially about how to do certain things and what materials and tools to use, which skilled workers almost always know and which unskilled or semiskilled workers seldom know. It has been found that actual skill and ability to answer these questions are highly correlated.

Examples of a few of these "trade-test" questions from each of several trades might be interesting:[5]

Milling Machine Operator

1. Q. What cutter is particularly adapted for milling thin castings that are likely to chatter?
   A. Helical tooth milling cutter.
2. Q. Where do you sharpen a gear (tooth) cutter?
   A. On face (between teeth).

Diesinker

1. Q. What is the end of the forging called where it is joined to the stock?
   A. Gate or sprue.
2. Q. What is a small curved file called?
   A. Riffler.

Molder, Iron and Brass

1. Q. Why is a pattern painted red in spots?
   A. To show the cores or core points.
2. Q. What are chaplets used for?
   A. Divide metal in cores.

There are, as a rule, from 15 to 20 questions for each trade. You will find it of value to get from the library the book from which these questions are taken or a similar book and either use the questions given in the book for the occupations you supervise or prepare your own lists.

An interviewer in an employment office is required to read the

[5] From *Interview Aids and Trade Questions for Employment Offices,* Lorin A. Thompson (Harper & Brothers).

questions from his card in the exact order given and to record whether or not the applicant answered each correctly.

Since you will be much more familiar with the occupations for which you are interviewing than is the office interviewer, you will be able to use a much less formal method.

For example, if you were interviewing an applicant for a job as milling machine operator, after the "warm-up questions," you might ask what makes and types of milling machines he operated in the shop he worked in last and what work he did. You might then ask if he had any trouble with thin castings to keep them from chattering and what he did to stop chatter. You might ask, also, if he sharpened his own cutters and if so what he considered the best method of sharpening a gear or tooth cutter. Similarly, other questions could be asked.

You should try to ask these questions as if you were discussing shop practice with another mechanic rather than giving an examination.

All of the important points should, however, be covered and if this cannot be done without direct questioning, do not hesitate to use direct questioning.

If an incorrect answer is given, it is usually better not to make any comment to that effect. If some unusual method is mentioned which you think might work, ask for fuller details. Often you may get some good suggestions.

8. *Avoid trick questions*

One representative of a large corporation when interviewing college seniors uses this question:

"In this business of ours, honesty is absolutely essential. Of course, I know you are honest, so I don't need to question you on that subject. But, by the way, why are you honest?"

If the student answers this question as to why he is honest to the satisfaction of the interviewer, the interview is continued. If he does not, the interview is closed promptly and the student is not considered.

If the student answers, "I am honest because I think honesty pays," that answer is considered incorrect and the person does not get the job.

Some such answer as "I am honest because my mother always

taught me to be honest and I believe it to be the right thing," or something to that effect, is considered more nearly correct and the interview is continued.

There may be some value to the use of questions of this type, but, as a rule, interpretation of the applicant's answers is so difficult that it is doubtful if the method should be used by any but trained psychiatrists, and many doubt the value even then.

9. *Listen attentively and show evidence of being interested*

I know an executive who actually turns his back and closes his eyes when he in interviewing. He does this so that he can concentrate on what the person is saying and he is a keen analyst, but he so disconcerts the applicant that it is impossible for any but the most self-assured to give a good account of himself and, as a result, the executive passes over many good people.

The interview should be a friendly "conversation with a purpose," and you should show the same animation and interest that you would if you were listening to some friend relating an interesting experience. Laugh with the applicant at his jokes or amusing experiences. There is no better way to get him to open up and reveal his true nature—whether this revelation is to his advantage or to his disadvantage.

10. *Talk only enough yourself to keep conversation informal and friendly; avoid expressing opinions or asking leading questions*

Avoid, especially, telling your own experiences except, possibly, in the opening moments.

There is a tendency—a thoroughly natural tendency—for the interviewer to want to "show off" just a little by telling something of his skill or some of his experiences demonstrating the high degree to which he has qualities about which he is talking. The temptations to do this are so insidious that only by conscious and constant effort and attention can the practice be avoided. I say this so positively because I know that in my own case it is the mistake I must guard against most carefully and because, in interviews I have heard, it is the most common failing.

In fact I have in several instances seen applicants win commendation from executives as "really knowing their stuff" when about all they did was to listen to the interviewer attentively and occasionally interject a comment indicating approval of what the interviewer was saying and admiration of how skillfully the interviewer had handled the situation in the story he was telling.

11. *Do not let the interview become mechanical; keep on the alert for unexpected evidence*

The interview should be systematic; otherwise all necessary points will not be covered. Care should be exercised, however, not to let it become mechanical. Often, after the discussion of one quality has been completed, the applicant will say something that throws new light on that quality and the interviewer must keep constantly on the alert for such occurrences.

It is natural that any applicant will endeavor to make the best possible showing in the interview and, when answering direct questions about any quality, will give only those facts which are favorable. However, after he thinks discussion of that quality is closed, he is somewhat off his guard and will tell incidents, possibly in supporting his claim for excellence in some other quality, which will give valuable evidence to be used in judging the former quality.

12. *After the close of the formal interview, watch for additional evidence*

After the close of the formal interview the conversation should drop back for a few moments into the friendly informal style with which it opened. This serves two purposes. It lets the applicant leave feeling more important, and therefore more friendly to the organization, than if there were an arbitrary close when the interviewer has finished questioning the applicant. Also, when the formal interview is over, the applicant will frequently relax his guard and relate some incidents or make some comments which reveal characteristics not revealed in the interview proper.

13. *Record your impressions and your reasons for them immediately after the person leaves—before starting the next interview*

Unless impressions and the facts that caused the impressions are recorded at once they will often be forgotten. This is especially true if several applicants are being interviewed. It is easy, and sometimes quite embarrassing, to forget which one said this and which said that. Even if no form is provided for recording this information, notes should be made in sufficient detail so that an accurate report can be dictated later, or the notes consulted when reaching a decision.

Any information as to the applicant's availability for appointment, changed address, added references, may be written during the interview.

14. *Provide for a second interview whenever practicable*

It seems almost uncanny how frequently important factors which were overlooked or which did not appear at all in the first interview will be observed in the second interview. This is especially true when the applicant has an unusually pleasing personality, which may cause the interviewer to overlook other significant factors. Sometimes these discoveries will be in the applicant's favor, sometimes against him. The timid or nervous applicant is more at ease and shows to better advantage; the scheming, self-confident applicant feels that he "has the job in the bag" and "loosens up" to his disadvantage. The interviewer, too, has had time to think about some points on which he did not get sufficient information and he can now get this.

A second interview is especially valuable when interviewing for important sales positions unless, of course, salesmen of the high-pressure, one-interview type are wanted. "Personality boys" who can sweep the interviewer off his feet in the first interview can seldom do this in the cold gray dawn of a second interview.

Even if the applicant comes from a distance and can remain only the one day, it as well to ask him to come in to see you again for a few moments before he leaves.

If There Is a Central Employment Office

Many supervisors who read this book will be in organizations where there are central employment offices. This does not by any means take away their responsibility for proper selection. The selection of employees is a partnership affair. Supervisor and employment manager are the partners. Each has his part, and each must do his part if there is to be successful selection.

The supervisor, when making his request for help, should state exactly what are the duties of the job, particularly any duties which may be either unpleasant or difficult. He should include any suggestions he may wish to offer as to age, schooling, experience, or personality; remembering, when preparing these specifications, to think of the actual job requirements and to eliminate any "hobbies" of his own.

If applicants are sent to him for interviews, he should attend to this as promptly as possible. A friendly greeting will put an applicant at his ease, and help to sell the organization and the department to him. Probably no one of the persons sent will measure up 100 per cent to the specifications. The employment office has done the best it can, but a 100 per cent applicant is not always available. Good personality, sufficient basic education, a liking for the work, and a desire to learn are probably much more important than mere experience. This is especially true of selling positions.

If the supervisor does feel it necessary occasionally to reject an applicant sent down by the employment office—and it is right that he should—he should be sure to let that office know promptly, by either note or telephone, exactly why he has felt it necessary to do this. This will enable the employment manager to avoid repeating the error. It is usually a good plan just to send the applicant back and to telephone the employment office, letting that office do the "turning down."

Whenever opportunity offers, the person in the employment office who does the interviewing should be shown the work that is done in a department and what the supervisor thinks are the general requirements for success. The more the employment interviewer knows about the department the better able will he be to select people who will really "make good."

Supervisors should be careful about making promises. Great care should be exercised in describing the possibilities so as not to exaggerate and not to say anything the applicant may misconstrue as a promise. I have often had employees come to me after a short period of employment and say that the supervisor or I had "definitely promised" a salary increase at that time; when all we had said was that it was *possible if the person showed unusual ability that he might be given an increase then.* When talking to applicants it should always be remembered that a perfectly general statement such as this will often be taken as a promise and hard feelings caused. No one can foresee the future well enough for it to be safe for him to make any distant promises. All that he can do is to endeavor to make an honest and conservative analysis of the possibilities, making it fully clear that such an analysis is not a promise.

It is better to have a reputation for actually developing and advancing people than it is to have one for making glowing promises.

Suggested Supplementary Reading on Interviewing

How to Interview, Bingham and Moore.

II. Learning How to Interview; IV. The Employment Interview.

An Approach to More Objective Oral Tests, Samuel H. Ordway, Jr., and James C. O'Brien.

This pamphlet, published by the Society for Personnel Administration of Washington, D.C., deals with a series of experiments which have sought to isolate certain essential factors of personal capacity that can be evidenced reliably through oral tests. The sections on, "Adduction of Evidence" and "Standards of Rating" are especially interesting.

Handling Personality Adjustment in Industry, Robert M. McMurry.

IX. Techniques of Employee Selection; XVI. Training the Employment Interviewer.

Psychiatry in Industry, V. V. Anderson.

VII. A Psychiatric Guide for Employment Interviewers; VIII. Qualities Distinguishing Good and Poor Sales Clerks.

CHAPTER VIII

Job Evaluation and Salary Administration

DETERMINING just how large a salary or wage each person in an organization is entitled to is one of the most difficult problems of management; and management needs the conscientious and thoughtful help of the supervisor in every step of the solution of that problem.

"In fixing wages or salaries, three points must be considered: First, what are the duties of the job; second, what is the value of these duties; third, how well does the employee perform these duties. We can condense the problem into three brief questions: 'What is the job?' 'What is it worth?' 'How well does he do it?' In addition, consideration must be given to prices prevailing in the competitive wage market."[1] The first of these questions is discussed in Chapter V; the third in Chapter XII. This chapter discusses the problems suggested by the second, and probably the most difficult of the questions is, What is the job worth?

Solution of these problems has been approached by several methods, the three best known being the Classification Plan, the Point Rating Plan, and the Factor Comparison Method.

THE CLASSIFICATION PLAN

The first step in the classification plan, as in other systematic attempts at job evaluation, is to prepare for each position in the organization a detailed statement of the duties of the position (see Chapter V).

Next, all positions are carefully grouped or "classified," first

[1] From *Manual of Job Evaluation*, Benge, Burk, and Hay (Harper & Brothers).

by *type of work done* (as, for example, accounting clerical or stenographic or legal) and then by *level of difficulty and responsibility* within each type of work (as junior accounting clerk, accounting clerk, and senior accounting clerk).

After the positions are thus classified, each is assigned to one salary range of a set of salary ranges. This set of ranges is either fixed by law as in many governmental services or by the management of the organization. The assignment of the different positions to the various salary range levels is usually made on the basis of carefully made community salary surveys. Suggestions on the preparation of salary ranges are given later in this chapter.

For each level of position in each type of work there is usually prepared a brief description of the duties considered of sufficient difficulty or responsibility to justify classification of the position in that level. For example, the summarized descriptions for the three levels of accounting clerical work mentioned above are as follows:

Junior Accounting Clerk

Following a set routine and specific directions, to do accounting-clerical work of a repetitive nature allowing little discretion. This work includes tasks such as: (a) the manual posting of records from media on which debits and credits to accounts are clearly indicated; (b) transcribing indicated accounting data to simple forms or statements; (c) making simple arithmetic calculations such as computing penalty interest; and (d) maintaining files of punch cards on which accounting data are recorded.

Accounting Clerk

Following specific rules and procedures involving a considerable variety of steps, to do accounting-clerical work which requires the exercise of some discretion or interpretation. This work includes tasks such as: (a) maintaining (including adjusting and balancing) accounting records from media on which debits and credits to accounts are indicated or obvious; (b) preparing forms or statements requiring the compilation of specified data from various accounting records; (c) preparing routine journal entries; (d) indicating the application of remittances in accordance with specific rules; (e) routine checking of forms of documents to determine completeness; and (f) supervising a small group of junior accounting clerks.

Senior Accounting Clerk

Applying general rules to a variety of cases, to do accounting-clerical work that allows considerable discretion or interpretation, or to supervise accounting-clerical work where the supervision requires thorough knowledge of the procedures involved, but requires little technical accounting knowledge. This work includes tasks such as: (a) maintaining (including adjusting and balancing) complex accounting records from various media; (b) preparing a variety of journal entries necessary to record routine transactions; (c) preparing financial reports requiring the selection and summarization of data from various bookkeeping records or media.

New Positions and Job Reclassification

When a new position is to be classified or a change in duties makes it desirable that the classification be reviewed, the follow ing steps are usually followed:

1. A carefully prepared duties statement is obtained in the manner described in Chapter V.

2. This statement is studied for "allocation factors," as the duties or responsibilities which are most significant in establishing the classification are called.

3. The brief discriptions of duties of possible classifications and duties statements of similar positions previously classified are studied.

4. The position in question is allocated to the class which the type of work and the difficulty and responsibility of the duties most closely match. This allocation to a class automatically sets the salary range because each class has previously been assigned a salary range.

The classification plan has worked satisfactorily in many organizations. It seems especially well suited to the governmental services. This means that it is sufficiently practical and defensible to stand the test of public scrutiny, and that is a good recommendation for its use in private organizations.

The Point Rating Plan

The point rating plan of job evaluation is probably the plan most widely used in private business. In this plan a number of factors or qualities common to all jobs in the organization are chosen. A schedule of point values is assigned to each of the variout gradations of each factor.

The system used by the Detroit Edison Company[2] will serve as an example.

"The Detroit Edison Company has adopted a point-rating plan for appraising occupations which has been successfully used by a number of companies in the electric power and light industry.

"The point-rating scale measures the relative value of occupations on the basis of five major factors. . . . Each of these major factors is subdivided into from two to four sub-factors, and the sub-factors are further graded into six degrees. Each degree is defined in general terms and is given a value in points. Every factor of the scale is given a weight which expresses its relative importance. These weights have been determined over a period of several years of use in public utility firms and are believed to be accurate for the industry.

"The major factors, sub-factors, and their weights are as follows:

Factor	*Weight*
A—*Responsibilities* (165)	
1. Responsibility for Supervision	100
2. Responsibility for Handling Confidential Matters	20
3. Responsibility for Safety of Others	25
4. Responsibility for Performance of Work without Immediate Supervisor	20
Total	165
B—*Knowledge, Skill and Experience* (80)	
5. Specialized or Professional Knowledge Required	30
6. Manual or Other Physical Skill Required	20
7. Company Experience Required	30
Total	80

[2] This description of the point rating plan of the Detroit Edison Company is quoted from the *Management Review* (American Management Association) of July, 1944, in which it is summarized from an article by Lynden J. Kaufmann in *Edison Electric Institute Bulletin.*

Factor	Weight
C—*Work Complexities* (110)	
8. Complexity and Difficulty of Work	90
9. Seriousness of Errors	20
Total	110
D—*Contacts* (70)	
10. Contacts with Customers or Other Companies	50
11. Contacts with Other Departments	20
Total	70
E—*Working Conditions* (40)	
12. Hazards	30
13. Irregularity of Hours and/or Adverse Working Conditions	10
Total	40
Grand Total	456

"Each sub-factor is defined as to scope, and the significance of each degree is explained in general terms.

"In rating occupations, the whole series of occupations under review is considered with respect to one factor at a time. If the factor applies to the occupation, the proper number of points is selected by reference to the table of degree definitions. When all factors have been completed, the points assigned to each kind of work are added, and the resulting total expresses the relative position of the work in the company as a whole."

Construction of wage and salary charts for the purpose of converting the numerical ratings into dollars and cents of pay, is accomplished through the medium of wage surveys.

The principal difficulty with point rating plans is in determining the correct maximum value in points for each factor.

On the whole, however, it is an excellent plan and has proved successful in actual use in a number of organizations.

THE FACTOR COMPARISON METHOD[3]

The factor comparison method of job evaluation was designed in an attempt to make use of the good points of the other systems and avoid some of their difficulties and possible inaccuracies.

[3] This description of the Factor Comparison Method is a summary of a fuller description given in *Manual of Job Evaluation*, by Benge, Burk, and Hay (Harper & Brothers).

1. The first step in installation is to prepare a detailed description of each job and a specification of the qualities needed for the job.

2. Next, as a basis for comparison, factors are selected which are common to all jobs. These are:

Mental Requirements
Skill Requirements
Physical Requirements
Responsibility
Working Conditions

3. The next step is to select 15 or 20 "key jobs," which are jobs clearly defined as to duties, whose rates are not subject to controversy, and which are not admittedly or comparatively underpaid or overpaid. These key jobs should vary in salary from the lowest to nearly the highest salaries paid in the organization.

4. The key jobs are then listed in order of rank from the highest to the lowest, *separately for each of the five factors.* This is done most carefully and the final result is the average of about thirty opinions.

A job such as *machine bookkeeper* will then appear thus:

	Rank in Importance
Mental Requirements	5th
Skill Requirements	5th
Physical Requirements	5th
Responsibility	4th
Working Conditions	5th

5. Next the typical or average salary for each of the key jobs is divided into five parts, assigning one part to each of the five factors in accordance with its estimated importance.

Thus the average pay of forty machine bookkeepers is $170 per month and the different factors are estimated to be worth:

Mental Requirements	$ 30.00
Skill Requirements	47.00
Physical Requirements	30.00
Responsibility	44.00
Working Conditions	19.00
	$170.00

It should be remembered that this is one of the key jobs, which are so chosen and named because the rates paid for them are generally agreed to be about right. In other words, the average salary of bookkeepers, $170, is considered to be the right one, based on long experience and study of salaries paid by competitors.

6. The results of step (5) are compared with step (4) and any discrepancies are eliminated by discussion. If there are any discrepanices which cannot easily be ironed out these jobs are eliminated from the key list. This gives, for each of the five factors, a rating scale, in points on which there is full agreement.

The rating scale of key jobs in this case for the factor *Mental Requirements* is as follows:

	Requirements
F—Messenger Boy	16
R—Income Tax Punch Card Operator	24
J—File Clerk	28
D—Machine Bookkeeper	30
B—Outside Collector	35
P-Q—Ediphone Op.—Unit Supv. Bkpg.	44
E—Teller	57
K—Remittance Clerk	70
L—Court Accountant	74
C—Head Bookkeeper	154

7. Now the committee of high-ranking operating officials and the job analysts compare all other jobs in the company with the key jobs. They place new jobs in correct order of rank for each of the five factors, one at a time, by comparing them with the key jobs on the rating scales for each factor.

Each job is compared with the key jobs on each factor, and given a value for the factor. Adding up the values for all factors gives the total point value for the job—discrepancies being smoothed out in committee. Finally, the results are submitted to the various departments for their criticism and approval.

The most important differences between the factor comparison method of job evaluation and the point rating plan are:

1. In the factor comparison method there are no fixed maximum or minimum limits to the point values set for each factor, nor is there any table with descriptions of gradations to be used in rating the job. The rating scale used consists of a number of

key jobs which have been most carefully rated on each factor. Rating of any job on any given factor is accomplished by comparing it with other actual jobs rather than with printed definitions. This makes more accurate ratings and ratings which may more easily be defended if they are challenged.

2. In most point rating plans it is necessary to have a conversion factor by which the point rating of any job must be multiplied to obtain the salary rate. In the factor comparison method each point is one dollar per month (or one cent per hour if the payment for key jobs is on this basis). This is automatically accomplished by the method used in establishing the rating scale.

Wage and Salary Administration

There are a few principles in the design of salary ranges which have been proved sound by experience.

The "spread" from lowest to highest salary to be paid for any one position should be about one-third of the minimum salary. For example, if the starting salary for a beginner is $150 a month, the maximum total salary increase the person may receive for length of service and increased efficiency in doing the same work should be about $50, making the maximum salary $200 a month. If the employee, because of his efficiency, takes on new duties or is given added responsibility, *the job itself* changes (rather than merely the person's efficiency on the job) and a new and higher *range* will be applicable.

The average amount of each salary increase should be about 6 per cent of the employee's salary rate before the increase. For a person getting $200 a month the logical increase for good service would, therefore, be to $212 and the next to $224.72 then to $237.50, etc.

However, it is generally accepted *that monthly salaries should be in multiples of $5.* When this practice is followed, salary increases of $5 a month are given until 6 per cent of monthly rate becomes closer to $10 than to $5, when the amount of the increases are changed to $10 and similarly to $15, $20, etc. In recent years, with the many deductions for taxes and other purposes making it impossible to have an even amount in the envelope, the advantages of having monthly rates set at multiples of

$5 seem largely to have vanished; but the practice still continues.

If these principles are followed, each range will have six different salary rates (five steps) from the lowest or beginner's rate to the top rate for that position. A typical range for a position beginning at $100 a month would be:

$100.00 $105.00 $110.00 $115.00 $125.00 $135.00

The determination of the salary range to which each position will be assigned is usually based on a community salary survey.

The first step in this is to prepare brief descriptions of twenty or more positions that are believed to be common to a number of businesses in the community. These should represent positions ranging from nearly the lowest to nearly the highest in salaries paid.

A member of the personnel office staff who is thoroughly familiar with the positions should then call on a number of representative firms and exchange information as to salaries paid.

The brief descriptions of duties are essential as job titles often mean quite different things in different organizations.

After the survey is completed, the average salary in the community for each position may easily be computed, omitting figures so different from the average as to indicate that they are either incorrect or represent isolated cases.

To decide on the proper range a good practical plan is, first, to choose from the General Salary Table on page 98 the salary nearest to the average, then to take the two salaries before and the three after it and use these six salary rates to make up the range for the position.

The method is based on the theory that the community average should be at the middle of our normal range, with one step extra put on the top to be used as a reward for outstanding efficiency or unusually long and faithful service. As an example, assume that the community average salary for senior accounting clerk is $246.50. The nearest salary in the table is $250. Taking the two salaries below and the three above gives the following range:

$220.00 $235.00 $250.00 $265.00 $280.00 $295.00

A general salary table, so designed that individual salary increases are approximately 6 per cent and the approximate spread between the minimum and maximum of each six-salary range is one-third, is given below:

General Salary Table

90	95	100	105	110
115	125	135	145	155
165	175	185	195	205
220	235	250	265	280
295	315	335	355	375
400	425	450	475	500

Salary Reviews. At regular intervals, certainly not less often than once a year, there should be a complete and careful review of each person's duties and his efficiency in the performance of these duties to decide whether or not he is entitled to a salary increase.

Whenever duties change so as to entitle any person to a change in the classification of his position, this change should be made immediately without waiting for the regular review, and if the resultant change to a new salary range entitles the person to a salary increase, this, too, should be given immediately.

Often, however, changes in duties, especially somewhat gradual changes, will be overlooked. For this reason each person's duties should be reviewed as a part of each salary review so that, if merited classification changes have been overlooked, they may be made at that time.

At that same time the general effectiveness of the person's service should be reviewed and rated (see Chapter XII).

As a general rule, salary increases should be limited to one step of the range, but in cases of unusually meritorious service, especially if the salary is below the middle of the range, two steps should be given.

No plan should be considered as an ironclad rule. While, in general, new employees should be started at the minimum of the range for the position to which they are appointed, and salary increases should be made only at review times and only in the amounts specified in the plan, it should always be remembered that the plan is set up as an aid to good management, not as a fixed set of rules none of which may be broken no matter what the conditions.

Qualified persons who have had years of experience in doing work similar to that for which they are being employed should be started at above the minimum. But great care should be taken in doing this not to upset employees who started at the minimum in your own organization some years previous to the employment of the new person and who may not yet have reached the salary at which you are planning to employ the new person.

Exceptions are so likely to cause upsets that many organizations make the rule that for any exception to the plan two conditions must be fulfilled:

1. There must be a written statement in the employee's file setting forth why the exception is recommended.

2. The recommendation must be approved by an official *one step higher* than would be necessary for a similar action *within the plan*. Thus, if the department foreman may approve the appointment of a new employee if the salary is at the minimum, approval of the general foreman would be required for an appointment at a salary above the minimum.

This is desirable because the whole value of the plan will be lost if too frequent exceptions are made. If frequent exceptions are necessary, something is wrong, either with the plan or with the management of the department. For example, if any department is constantly requesting appointments at higher than the minimum, the range may be too low or the training and promotion program of the department may be at fault.

Suggested Supplementary Reading on Job Evaluation and Salary Administration

Manual of Job Evaluation, Benge, Burk, and Hay.

Probably the best available book giving detailed descriptions of the application of procedures of job analysis and appraisal in private business.

A detailed, step-by-step description is given of how the Factor Comparison Method of job evaluation was installed in one organization.

Position Classification in the Public Service, Ismar Baruch and a Committee.

This book, prepared by a committee of the Civil Service Assembly under the able chairmanship of Mr. Ismar Baruch of the United States

Civil Service Commission, is the most complete description of every phase of position classification available.

While it is prepared especially for the public service, it contains many suggestions of equal value to job analysts and classifiers in private business.

Clerical Position Evaluation Plan.

This booklet describes the plan used on all clerical positions with Revere Copper and Brass, Inc., of Rome, N. Y. The factors considered and the maximum values are:

1. Elemental Factor Value (including neatness, dependability, personality, etc.)	45 points
2. Educational Requirements	16 points
3. Practical Experience Required	15 points
4. Analytical Requirement and Complexity of Work	15 points
5. Accuracy	8 points
6. Memory	8 points
7. Manual Dexterity	5 points
8. Supervisional Requirements	15 points
9. Conditions of Work	5 points
10. Continuity of Work	5 points
11. Physical Strain on Senses	5 points
12. Relations or Contacts	8 points

Job Evaluation, Otis and Leukart

The four basic systems of job evaluation are described and the advantages of each discussed in considerable detail.

CHAPTER IX

Getting the New Employee Off to a Good Start

"SELECTING the worker for a certain kind of work and bringing him into productive relationship with it are two entirely different things. In order to bridge the gap, we must introduce the worker to his work. We must impart to him that information, that confidence, and that point of view which will transform him from an accepted applicant who, nevertheless, is usually ill at ease, into a capable worker, confident and interested."[1]

The first few days of almost anyone on a new job are difficult and trying, especially if he is taking up a new type of work. Any word of welcome and encouragement the supervisor may be able to give the new worker will count much in building that loyalty to the organization so necessary to the best work. And, conversely, any careless or unjust criticism or any indication of dissatisfaction at how inexperienced the new worker is may create a sore spot which will take months to heal.

More can be done to make or mar the new employee's future in the first few days than in weeks at any other time.

Even though you may have assigned the training of the new employee to an assistant, you should take time yourself to make the new person feel at home. This need not take much time. Often just a thoughtful word, said at the right time, will be all that is necessary. An incident that occurred during my own college days will serve to illustrate this point.

I had been forced to drop out of school quite young, because of family finances, but in seven years had saved up enough to

[1] From *Personnel Management*, Scott, Clothier, Mathewson, and Spriegel (McGraw-Hill Book Co.).

begin again. I first spent a year and a half making up my deficiencies in preparatory work and taking some freshman work in a college in my own home town in Florida where I was, of course, well acquainted with the people and where everything was pleasant. I had read about the new co-operative courses in engineering which Dean Herman Schneider had started in the University of Cincinnati, and I decided that this was the real way to learn engineering, so I went to Cincinnati and after two months of practical work I entered the engineering college with enough advanced credit so that I hoped to complete the five-year course in four years.

The first few weeks were gloomy ones. One day in particular I was about to give up. We had just moved into the uncompleted engineering building, and everything was upset. It was one of those cold days with half rain, half mist that penetrates everything. The campus was a sea of mud, as there had been no time to sod it after the construction. My bank account had dwindled down to just $120, not much to carry one through four years, and I knew my parents were unable to help me. I was walking along the plank walk from the engineering building to the chemistry laboratory wondering if, after all, I wanted a college education, when I heard someone walking briskly behind me, and a cheery voice said:

"Well, Halsey, this isn't much like Florida weather, is it?"

I looked around. It was Dean Schneider. I had read in the magazines so much about Dean Schneider and his wonderful work there that he was as big to me as the President of the United States. And he remembered my name, and where I was from, and took the trouble to speak to me.

It may have continued to rain and I know the campus was muddy for many a day, but it never worried me again. Somehow, too, the slim bank balance lasted, so that when four years later the same Dean Schneider handed me my diploma, the money was not quite all gone.

Perhaps the most important single moment in the induction process is that in which you, as the new employee's supervisor, receive him from the employee counselor or representative of the employment office who has brought him to your department. Here are two examples. In both cases the supervisor is busy with something important and cannot, at the moment, do more than say a few words.

In the first case, Bill Hastings was the supervisor. Charlie Williams, the assistant employment manager, brought the new employee into the department shortly after opening time. Bill had talked to him when he was being considered for the job, but seemed to have forgotten this. The assistant employment manager opened the conversation:

"Hello, Bill, I brought you the new man I promised you. Mr. Johnson, this is your new supervisor, Mr. Hastings. I believe you talked with Mr. Johnson before, Bill."

Bill made no comment to indicate that he remembered the interview, but addressed his remarks to Charlie.

"You sure can bring new people at the time when I am most busy, Charlie. He will have to wait a while until I have time to get him started. Has he ever operated a milling machine?"

"No, Bill, but I am sure he will learn quickly. He had a high score on the tests."

"Maybe; but teaching takes time and I am mighty busy with more important things now. I wish you would bring me some one once in a while who has had some experience. I'll take care of getting him started as soon as I can, I have to get this new job on the machines first."

Charlie showed the new man to a seat near Bill's desk, and left him with the comment: "Don't worry about Bill's comments. He is not half so bad as he sounds. He really is a good scout."

In the second case Jim Swain was the supervisor. Immediately after leaving Bill's department Charlie took Sam Williams, another new man, to Jim's department. Jim was too busy and could give only a short time at the moment to greeting the new employee; but here is how he handled it. Charlie started in the same way as before:

"Hello, Jim, here is the new man I promised you. Mr. Williams, this is your new supervisor, Mr. Swain."

"You don't need to introduce me to Mr. Williams, we had a long talk together a few days ago," and turning to the new employee, "I believe you said your first name is Sam, didn't you? We go by first names around here. Mine is Jim, as I told you. As I remember it, you have never run a turret lathe, but don't let that worry you; from the way Charlie tells me you handled his tests I am counting on you to be one of our best men in a short time. I have got to get this new job in the machines right now, but I will be with you in a little while. Just sit down over by my desk. You can be reading that book about the company they gave you in the employment office. . . . Will you show Jim where the desk is, Charlie?"

Assuming that the two new employees are of equal ability and the jobs of equal difficulty, and that each is turned over to a competent mechanic to be trained, how much longer will it take to transform the first man into "a capable worker, confident and interested" than it will take to do the same for the second man? An exact answer is impossible, but it will definitely be a considerable period of time—good productive time wasted because the supervisor was so busy getting out production that he didn't have time to be pleasant. And the interesting part of it all is that it probably took as much of Bill's time to explain why he didn't have time to be pleasant as it did for Jim to be pleasant. It usually does.

When *you* are the supervisor and *your* assistant employment manager brings you a new employee at just the moment when everything else seems to need your attention, whose handling of the situation does your greeting of the new employee most closely resemble, that of Bill Hastings or that of Jim Swain?

Objectives of the Process of Introducing the Worker to His Job

To give the new employee a feeling of confidence in himself

Perhaps the most important objective in introducing the employee to his new work and surroundings is to eliminate as quickly as possible that feeling of awkwardness and ignorance which makes him feel so inferior to those around him. The process is simple. First, greet him pleasantly and introduce into the greeting a word of assurance that you believe he will learn quickly. Second, see that someone shows him pleasantly and promptly those little things a worker must know, such as location of washrooms, drinking fountains, lunchroom; how to get tools or supplies when needed, how to record his time properly, how to get any money he may need to tide him over until his first pay day. Third, follow up frequently through the training period with a friendly word of encouragement, commenting especially on those parts of the work he is doing well and offering real instruction as to how he can do better those parts he is not doing quite so well. If each supervisor could understand how fully the thoughts and feelings of most new employees are dominated by doubts and fears and how great is the hunger for an occasional word of reasurance, labor turnover in the first few weeks would be greatly reduced and the whole training process speeded and made more efficient.

To make sure that he has complete knowledge of the conditions of his employment

It is primarily the responsibility of the employment office to make sure that each new employee knows exactly how much he is to be paid for regular time and overtime; understands any wage incentive plan, and is fully informed as to any bonuses for perfect attendance or penalties for absence or tardiness; but the new employee is told so much on that first day that he will probably not remember some of the conditions until he finds himself losing out on a bonus or being penalized in some other way. The supervisor can usually obviate such unpleasant experiences by taking a few moments to explain these things again to the new employee.

To give him an understanding of the importance of observing safety rules

This objective is discussed in Chapter XXII.

To give him a feeling of pride in "his company," "his shop," or "his store"

The employment office will probably give the new employee booklets describing the company—its history, the excellence of its products, the thrift and pension plans. The supervisor's part is, by question and comment, to make sure that the employee reads and understands the booklets, especially that he understands exactly how any of these plans benefit him or his family.

The new employee should be made proud of the product his company puts out. In one company there is a large showroom where the machines manufactured are displayed and there are photographs on the wall showing the important part these machines play in the manufacture of some world-famous products. After the new employee has been working a few days and his own feeling of awkwardness is wearing off, the supervisor takes him to the showroom and describes the machines to him, shows him the pictures, and, most important of all, points out to him just where the pieces he is helping to make are located in the machines and what is their purpose. The new employee soon begins to brag on the outside about "his company."

Suggested Supplementary Reading on Getting the New Employee off to a Good Start

Selecting and Inducting Employees, George D. Halsey.
Chapter XXI, Starting the New Worker on His Job.

Personnel Management, Scott, Clothier, and Spriegel.
Chapter 19, Introducing the Worker to His Job.

Orienting the New Worker, published by the Policyholders Service Bureau of the Metropolitan Life Insurance Company.
Describes in considerable detail the induction programs of several well-known organizations.

CHAPTER X

The Supervisor as a Teacher

> *The Law of Learning*
>
> Any connection, nervous or mental, that has once been made tends to recur.
>
> The strength of that tendency depends upon the INTENSITY, FREQUENCY, and RECENCY of the connection in past experience.

ABOUT half the average supervisor's work is teaching, in some form, and, usually, the larger the department supervised and the more complex the nature of the work done, the greater the percentage becomes. And this teaching is an important part of the supervisor's work, because through teaching the supervisor imparts to others the knowledge and skill he possesses and multiplies his own power to accomplish the desired results. Teaching can also largely eliminate the need for correction and discipline. Most mistakes are caused by lack of knowledge or lack of interest, and both are corrected by really skillful teaching.

Yet few supervisors have made any specific preparation for this part of their work. The reason is, probably, that most textbooks and articles on the subject deal in terms of classroom teaching and are often too theoretical to be of interest to the busy supervisor.

The general principles of teaching are here summarized in the form of fifteen practical suggestions applied directly to the teaching problems of the supervisor in shop, office, or store. Each has as its primary purpose increasing the speed and effectiveness of the learning process by the application of one or more of the three conditions given in the "Law of Learning"—Intensity, Frequency, Recency of the impression. Of the three, Intensity is the most important. If the impression is made deep and clear and true in the first place, much of the labor of reviewing, checking, and correcting will be avoided.

The Fifteen Suggestions

1. *Know the subject yourself*

The first requirement for success in teaching is to know clearly, accurately and completely that which you wish to teach.

2. *Try to have undivided attention*

The ideal condition is to have those you wish to teach in a room away from the noise of the shop or store; but this is not always practicable, especially in teaching such things as the operation of a machine or the arrangement of stock in a department. Try, however, to avoid distractions as much as you can.

There are certain simple devices for holding the attention and these should be used regularly. An important one which the supervisor-teacher can almost always use is to have something for those being taught to look at. If you are talking about a piece of merchandise, have the merchandise there, hold it up, turn it around; call attention to this point or that. If it is a new machine or device, have the article or at least a large photograph or blueprint.

Another important rule for holding attention in spite of distractions is to keep moving right along. Never drop your audience while you go to find that other blueprint or piece of merchandise, you intended to show. If you do, you will probably see that the thoughts of the group have wandered far afield. Plan to have everything you are to talk about right at hand. It should not, however, be in too plain view, because some members of the group will be looking at it and wondering what you are going to say about it, before you are ready for them to do this.

3. *Make the learner want to know*

The good teacher will always "sell his subject." Many teachers believe that they can afford to spend as much as 50 per cent of the available teaching time in arousing interest in the subject, and only 50 per cent in actual "instruction," and yet do a more successful job of teaching than if they spent the whole, or nearly the whole, time just stating the facts. This is true no matter how clearly the facts are stated. "Teaching is not filling a bucket; it is lighting a lamp." If you can arouse in those you would teach a real desire to know more about the subject you are teaching, the rest of your task is comparatively easy. In fact, with an alert adult group the "information-giving" part of teaching may, in some cases, even be omitted. If the interest is sufficiently aroused, they will find a way to get the information. As a rule, however, a fair balance between arousing interest and giving information should be maintained, a safe proportion usually being 30 per cent arousing interest or "selling" and 70 per cent giving information. But it should always be remembered that even the giving of information should be done in a manner that does not cause interest to wane.

Causing the employee to become interested in his work and keeping him interested in it are important in so many parts of personnel supervision that a brief discussion of what interest is and just what causes a person to find one activity more interesting than another will be of value.[1]

Any of the following conditions will, when they are present, tend to make an activity more interesting:

1. The activity has appeal and challenge because of its inherent difficulty and, when the activity is satisfactorily completed, there is, therefore, a sense of pride in having really accomplished something.

2. The activity is a natural one for the person and, therefore, done without great effort. The person who naturally and easily does any one thing better than most of his associates can do it, likes to do that thing.

3. The person believes that by doing the thing he will win the approval or even the applause of his associates.

4. The person has a feeling that the activity is accomplishing something of value and importance.

5. There has been freedom of choice. The person feels that he

[1] The discussion of interest that follows is largely a summary of a fuller discussion given in Chapter XIV of *Personnel Administration*, by Tead and Metcalf (McGraw-Hill Book Co.).

is doing this particular thing because he wants to do it, not because he is told that he must do it.

The alert supervisor-teacher will endeavor, by the methods of supervising and teaching he uses, to make sure that as many as possible of these conditions are present in the work of each employee under his supervision.

Whether the work is interesting or monotonous to the worker is determined not so much by the nature of the work itself as by how the work is presented to him, and often by whether or not the worker likes his supervisor. Just as one's interest in a subject in school can be changed completely when a different method of presentation is used, so a worker's whole attitude toward his work and his interest in it can be changed by improved methods of supervision.

Few jobs are so monotonous that they cannot, with proper teaching and supervision, be made interesting to an employee whose aptitudes and capacities fit the job. But even when boredom is a hazard, a skillful supervisor can introduce conditions into the work relationships which will make the combination of work and work relationship interesting. This is not always easy, but it can be done.

4. *Start with the known; lead into the unknown*

All teaching should start with that which is known. This at once captures the attention and gives all, teacher and those being taught, a common starting point. For example, the description of a new screw machine may begin:

"The new machine is similar to, but has one important difference from, the #47 which we are now using. You will remember that, on #47, when the operation gets to this point (holding up a piece of work or a blueprint and pointing to the place) the machine stops and the operator must turn the turret by hand. In the new design a cam has been introduced here (show large blueprint) etc."

The description of a new style just being introduced may begin:

"You all remember the so and so shoulder which was so popular last year, don't you, the one which came to a decided point, etc? The new shoulder line is somewhat similar to that, but, etc."

Do not use technical terms without first explaining them. Words that are everyday English to those of us who have spent many years in one type of business will be foreign to the average person from the outside, even though that person is well educated. It is best at the beginning to assume that the learner has no knowledge of the subject at all. You can then find out quickly how much he really does know, and modify the instruction accordingly.

5. *Teach the simple first, and lead up to the complicated*

Any new subject or process is difficult at first. If you try to launch right into the more difficult part of what you have to teach, you are likely to discourage the beginner. If you begin with the simpler things and make sure that they are mastered before we go into the complex, there will be much less discouragement. If it is possible to do so in your department, it will be well to choose the simplest work and let all new employees begin there. Then, after they master this, they can be taught the more complex parts.

Keep the new employee progressing into the more complex, however, just as rapidly as his ability will permit, because, if the process becomes too easy, he will be inclined to think that he has mastered the whole thing and that real effort is no longer necessary. In other words, try to gauge the speed of your teaching so that it constantly calls on the learner to give his best, but never goes beyond his ability.

6. *Keep your explanation to the point*

Avoid giving unrelated incidents and details, even if interesting, because the learner's attention will be taken off the main subject. Shall we let Major Hoople's father (from Ahern's famous cartoon "Our Boarding House") illustrate our point?

"Let me see, now—was it in '98? No—that was the year I broke my leg in Singapore—Yep, that's right, because I was first mate with Cap Nelson on the 'India Star'—no, it was th' 'Scotch Mist'—yeh—one-eyed Hogan used to play the concertina on it—no, by Joe, it was th' mouth-harp—sure, I remember buying it for him—no, I traded a parrot for it, with a Swede sailor—or was he a Dane? Nope—well, anyway—Say, what was I talking about?"

"Gosh, I forget!" was the answer. "Start on something else, but ride straight this time and quit taking those side trips!"

Probably none of us has ever been so guilty of rambling as is Mr. Hoople, Senior; but we all are sometimes guilty of letting this or that remind us of something which happened when we were in the market the last time, or when we worked in the steel mill, or were camping last summer—incidents which, although interesting, do not really contribute anything to the learner's understanding of the subject or to the probability of his remembering. It is, however, an excellent practice, wherever possible, to illustrate each more important point by a story, if the story will actually make the meaning clearer and will cause the learner to remember the point. Illustrations of this kind are a definite help to teaching. Use them frequently, but be sure that they really illustrate and not merely amuse.

And remember, "Ride straight and don't take any side trips."

7. *Give a reason for each step*

We remember anything much better if we know the reason why and, even in a simple process, there is always a reason why it is better to do it one way than another.

A second advantage in giving a reason is that any fact is more interesting when the learner knows the reason for it. Attention and all learning depend largely on interest.

A third advantage is that, if the learner knows the reason, he is much less likely to think some other way "just as good" and, thus, to get started in wrong methods, making the teaching of the correct method doubly hard and, sometimes, making discipline necessary.

The method used in presenting this principle of good teaching is an illustration of the principle itself. Three reasons are given why reasons should be given. It is for the reader to judge how much this increases the probability of his remembering and using this principle.

8. *Demonstrate by doing (or having done) correctly and exactly what the learner will later be asked to do*

Be sure the learner can see every move, every part of the work being demonstrated. One important detail to be remembered when demonstrating anything done with the hands is to face the same way the learner does. When you stand facing toward him your left hand is opposite his right hand and confusion in his mind as to which hand to use for each part of the operation is almost certain to result.

Go as slowly as is necessary for every detail to be seen and understood. Often you will have done the particular thing you are teaching so frequently that it has become a habit for you to do it rapidly, and unless you are careful you will have a tendency to do it just as rapidly when showing the process to the learner. Try to avoid this. Go slowly and make sure, by calling attention to it as you do it, that the learner sees each step. Be careful, however, not to go so slowly that the learner becomes bored and attention wanders. Check frequently to see that each step is seen and understood, and go just as rapidly as the learner can go, no faster, no slower.

Perform the operation the correct way only. Explain *briefly* why it is the correct way, and that other ways may cause confusion or damage; *but do not show how NOT to do the job.*

9. *Encourage discussion, especially questions*

One of the most important requirements for success in teaching, especially the type of teaching that the supervisor will usually be called upon to do, is to have the person being taught feel perfectly free to interrupt at any time to ask a question. Even though no question is asked, this feeling of freedom to ask puts the person in the proper frame of mind to learn. Especially when training a new employee, be sure that at an early stage of his training there is given the assurance that he should feel free, at any time, to ask questions. Explain to him that it is much better for him to ask ten questions, even if some of them are foolish questions, than to make one serious mistake.

10. *Promptly after each operation has been explained and demonstrated to the learner, give him an opportunity to demonstrate the operation as if he were teaching you—making sure that he understands and explains to you the reasons for each step*

This is probably the most important suggestion of all. When you explain just how to do a thing, even if your explanation is understood perfectly, the desired impression is established only slightly. Even when you demonstrate by doing the thing yourself, the impression still may be far from what you wish it to be. But when the learner is given a chance to do it and to explain it himself, the impression is greatly strengthened and, also, you have had an opportunity to make sure that your explanation and demonstration have been understood. The learner may feel sure that he understands and express confidence in his ability when you ask him; but when he attempts to do the thing himself or to explain it back to you, you will often find that he has misunderstood or forgotten some important part.

An amusing incident in the writer's home some years ago illustrates the importance of this commandment. A new maid, with no more than her share of intelligence, had been employed. She was supposed to go downstairs earlier than the family and, among other tasks, to bring in the milk. The side door had a thumb bolt and a regular lock. She was shown before she went to bed how both must be unlocked, and said that she understood.

The next morning the milk was not in; she could not unlock the door.

That night she was shown again most carefully just how to do it, and seemed to understand. The next morning the milk was still on the outside. The door was too much for Jane.

That evening one of the younger members of the family, who had been trained as a teacher, decided to apply some of her principles of teaching. She showed the maid carefully how it was done, then said, "Now, Jane, see if you can do it." After some fumbling and a little further coaching, Jane did it. The door was then locked, and Jane told to try again. She did much better, and after two or three trials she could do it quite well.

The next morning the milk was inside.

11. *Never forget that the emotions play an important part*

There is an emotional state that is most conducive to learning. It is important that the supervisor understand this and endeavor to bring about and maintain that state.

Feeling toward the information. The words "enthusiastic interest and a desire to know" sum up the feeling the supervisor should endeavor to bring about. This was discussed under "*Make the learner want to know.*"

Feeling toward the teacher. "Respect without fear" should be the feeling here. Encouraging the learner to ask questions is one way to bring this about. The supervisor must, also, be careful never to laugh at the learner's mistakes, if he would maintain this feeling. There is no place in any training program for sarcasm or ridicule. The learner will undoubtedly ask some foolish questions, but if the supervisor laughs at them or makes some sarcastic comment, the learner will "close up like a clam" and ask no more questions. Unless each person under your supervision looks upon you as a friend and counselor, one to whom he can come with all his questions and be sure of a sympathetic answer, you will not make a real success as a teacher or *as a supervisor.*

Nothing makes the right sort of person work harder than an occasional word of praise. If an employee does some particular thing exceptionally well, tell him so. Of course, you must be careful to give praise only when deserved, when something has been done better than usual, because if you get into the habit of praising almost everything that is fairly good, your praise will be cheap and the learner will not value it highly.

Criticism should also be given when deserved; but, when criticising adversely anything the employee has done, always give constructive advice as to how he may avoid making the same error again. And be careful, whenever possible, to give your criticism privately so that no one else hears.

12. *Check from time to time to see how well the information is retained and used*

Every supervisor knows how important a part of his work is that represented by the word "follow-up." This is as true of teaching as of any other part of his work. Much of any teacher's time is spent, and profitably spent, in reviewing what he has taught.

Having the employee do something that involves a use of the knowledge or ability gained is a better method of review than direct quizzing, because it shows not only that he possesses the necessary information, but also that he knows how to use it. The direct question or request for demonstration should also be used, however, without hesitation or apology, especially during the early stages of the training process.

Your check should go beyond being assured that the person knows or even that he knows how to do; there should be some method of checking to see whether or not he is actually using the information in his everyday work. If the learner is a saleswoman, does she present her merchandise in the manner taught; does she use skillfully in her sales talk the information about fashion, workmanship, color? If the learner is a machinist, is he following instructions accurately with each piece of work which goes into his machine, and not merely when the foreman asks for a demonstration of how the job should be done?

As a supervisor you are not only responsible for what the person knows, you are also responsible for what he does with what he knows. And that, after all, is the best test of the excellence of any teaching.

13. *Remember the importance of example as a teaching force*

Imitation is still a most important educational force. It should always be remembered that the learner is much more likely to imitate the leader's example than to follow his precept. If the two contradict each other, it will be difficult, indeed, to do a good job of teaching.

The supervisor should do whatever he does—operating any machine, stock work, selling, clerical work—exactly as he would have those under his supervision do it.

14. *Plan your teaching in advance*

Even the simplest teaching is done better if there is some advance planning. For meetings, important corrective interviews, and other more formal teaching, the plan should be in writing. For simpler teaching, just a quick mental review of the more important points will serve. At first, and until the habit of systematic planning is firmly fixed, it will be found helpful to have typed on a card six or seven questions similar to those below, and to use this card as a guide both in more elaborate written plans and in "quick" planning for the giving of simple instructions.

1. Exactly what do I want to teach; do I have it clearly in mind?
2. Why should the other person want to know; what advantage is there to him?
3. How can I show this advantage, quickly, simply?
4. What does he already know that is similiar?
5. What method will be best to use in teaching the unknown in terms of the known?
6. What is the best "follow-up," to be sure that the information is understood and correctly used in his everyday work?

Persistent following of this practice, *without exception*, for a brief time will form the habit of planning in this way, and soon it will be done almost unconsciously before even the simplest bit of teaching; and the executive will find that his instructions are being carried out much more accurately, and his own time and patience are being saved.

15. *Use the same care, the same teaching technique, in giving instructions to an individual*

Too often, instructions to an individual are given much more hastily than would be the case if these instructions were given to a group. It is unfair to any employee to expect intelligent co-operation unless all necessary instructions are given fully, clearly, and with due regard for that person's feelings. The same basic principles that apply to all teaching apply to the giving of even the simplest instruction to an employee. Much need for discipline and for doing things over would be eliminated if instructions were always given this way; and in the end the supervisor's time would be saved. A simple formula for giving instructions to an individual is:

Tell how and why.
Do the thing yourself.
Let the learner do it.
Check frequently and tactfully.

Adults Can Learn

For centuries the belief was held, even by professional teachers, that after a person had reached the age of thirty or forty it was extremely difficult, if not impossible, for him to learn new things.

But both academic research and the experience of thousands of training directors and supervisors have proved that adults, even adults well past middle age, *can* learn. Whether or not they *will* learn depends to a larger extent than with children on how the teaching is done. Both the method of teaching and the teacher's manner must take into account at least two important differences between mature adults and younger people.

Motivation is even more important

Before most adults will, *or even can*, give their best efforts to learning anything, they must be shown clearly *why they should want to learn that thing*—how, specifically, the new knowledge or skill will benefit them.

There is a strong tendency as a person grows older and older to require more and more definite and concrete motivation. He becomes less and less interested in learning because some future benefit is promised or just because the "teacher" says it is a thing he should know. It becomes increasingly necessary, therefore, that he be shown just what the knowledge or skill will do for him *now*.

Adults resent more strongly being "talked down" to

Another important difference between adult and younger learners which the teacher of adults must constantly keep in mind is that adults, especially those with years of trade or business experience, resent more strongly than do younger people being "talked down" to in the all too typical teacher-pupil manner. As a person grows older, he is likely to become increasingly sensitive about exposing ignorance of things he fears others think he should know. That is why it is often so difficult, when ordinary teaching methods are used, to introduce new or improved ways of doing things to a group that includes persons who have had long experience in the work. The cause is not so much any inherent inability to learn on the part of the older employee as it is an unconscious protection of the individual's pride, combined often with a fear that the new method may affect his job security—both most important considerations with the older worker.

A teaching method should be found that both protects the pride of the older worker and assures him that learning the new method improves rather than hurts his job security.

Suggested Supplementary Reading on Training

Training Employees, George D. Halsey

Chapter headings are as follows: Purpose and Importance of Training; General Teaching Principles Applied to Training; The Basic Training Pattern; The Conference as a Training Method; Guided Discussion; Other Training Methods and Devices; Use of Visual Aids in Training; Induction of New Employees and Information Booklets; How to Make Employee Meetings Interesting and Profitable; Training Industrial Workers; The Apprenticeship Plan for Skilled Workers; Training Office Workers; Training in Retail Stores; Training Outside Salesmen; Training for Promotion; Fitting the College Graduate into the Organization; Improving Employee Attitudes; Training in Safety; Determining the Training Needs and Planning the Program; Measuring the Effectiveness of the Training Program.

Adult Interests, by E. L. Thorndike.

Especially, Chapter XII, Methods of Teaching Adults.

Psychology for Executives, E. D. Smith.

Especially, Appendix I, which discusses the author's teaching methods.

Personnel Administration, Tead and Metcalf

Especially, Chapter XIII, The Training of Employees, and Chapter XIV, Arousing Interest in Work. The latter chapter, while not specifically on teaching methods, is of especial interest to the supervisor in his duties as a teacher, because of the great importance in teaching of causing the learner to want to know.

How to Train Supervisors, R. O. Beckman.

Outline 17, Training Employees. Outline 18, How to Demonstrate a Job. Outline 19, The Teaching Steps Analyzed.

CHAPTER XI

How To Hold a Good Meeting

"Learning without interest of some sort does not occur to any appreciable degree."—*E. L. Thorndike.*[1]

WERE you ever a member of an adult class in Sunday school where the program was about like this?

"Has anyone the attendance cards? Oh, there they are on the chair. Mr. Smith, will you call the roll?" Then the collection was taken; next, the teacher passed out the lesson leaves and asked Mr. Brown to read the first verse and Mr. Jones to read the comment on that verse. At about the middle of the session the Sunday-school secretary came for the attendance record and collection. The collection envelope could not be located at first, but after a little search it was found that Mr. Smithers, a late arrival, was sitting on it. In spite of all these interruptions the lesson was over and everyone was waiting to go before the first bell rang.

You may also have had the good fortune to have been a member of a Bible class where the room, although it was a big room, was so crowded that those who were late had trouble in finding seats. The attendance record was kept, the collection was taken, but all so unobtrusively that these things did not detract from the program at all. The Sunday-school secretary came around for the attendance cards and collection, but he found them in a pocket in the door. After a stirring hymn, the teacher stood up and quietly asked some thought-provoking question about the application of the lesson to everyday life. In a few moments discussion was so active that about all the teacher had to do was to keep it in proper channels. The first bell for

[1] From *Adult Interests*, E. L. Thorndike (The Macmillan Co.).

closing seemed to ring all too soon and the teacher summed up the discussion.

The difference between the two meetings was, most of all, in the planning and preparation. True, the second teacher probably had more natural skill in the art of being interesting; but, more often than not, the real difference between a dull, flat, uninteresting meeting and one in which you enjoy every moment is in the amount of work someone has put into it.

Any meeting can be made interesting. This is especially true of a meeting of employees, such as you as a supervisor will most frequently be called upon to conduct, since the information you wish to present usually has to do directly with the employees' success in the organization. You should not, however, let this advantage make you think it unnecessary to endeavor to apply every method you can to make your meetings even more interesting than the subject matter alone would make them. There are some simple methods and devices, used by many successful speakers and teachers, which you can use to advantage.

A good meeting, whether a Sunday-school class, a meeting of a society or club, a mass meeting of all of the employees of an organization, or just the gathering together of a small group of employees for the regular weekly meeting of the department, usually has behind it careful planning and preparation. No natural skill as a speaker or discussion leader can take the place of this, nor should any lack of skill or experience deter one from holding meetings. Anyone who knows his subject, possesses enthusiasm, and is willing to put a little hard work into the preparation can hold a good meeting.

Preparation

The purpose

First, before any material is assembled or any other preparation is made, there should be a clear and definite answer to the question, What do I want to accomplish by this meeting or series of meetings? And this answer should always be in terms of what you want people to be caused to do, rather than in terms of your desire to present a certain idea or teach a certain thing. The type of meeting in which you as a supervisor are most interested practically always has as its purpose the causing of some action. You want your employees to follow the safety rules of the shop; you want the salespeople in your department to present their merchandise in a way that will make the customer wish to own it; or you want your stenographers to be more careful in the spelling, punctuation, and grammar of the letters they send out. And you want these things to be done willingly and enthusiastically, not just because you, as the supervisor, say that they must be done.

This is so important that considerable time and thought should be given to it. It is relatively easy to plan a trip if you know exactly where you wish to go, but quite difficult if you have only some vague idea. The same is true of planning a meeting.

The listeners' wants

So far, we have considered only what *you* as the leader of the meeting wish to accomplish; but, as you remember from the discussion in Chapter III, the only way in which you can get this done is to relate it to something your listeners want and to show how doing what you want will get for them what they want. An important step in the preparation, then, is to think of and preferably to write down what the thing you plan to talk about will do for the listeners. Will it make their work simpler or more pleasant; will it help them to avoid errors which are embarrassing to them; will it help them to earn more money; will it enable them to win recognition or praise; will it give them added security? If it will do any of these or any similar things, that fact should be worked into the meeting plans.

The leader's knowledge

The leader of any meeting should know much more about his subject than just that part which he expects to teach. It is always dangerous to try to teach too close to the "edge" of one's knowledge. One may fall overboard and flounder around, and that spoils the meeting. Always prepare much more than you intend to use; you can use it later.

Properties

If a small machine or part or some merchandise is to be discussed, have a sample or samples at the meeting. There should, however, be as little confusion or delay as possible in showing the articles. If, for example, several articles are to be shown and they are so placed that you must walk across the room to get each new article, the interest of the group will be lost at each trip and must be recaptured each time. The show must be so well planned that it will move along smoothly, continuously.

Things to be shown to the group should, if possible, be out of sight until they are ready for use. One home-demonstration agent, who showed a number of bottles of various sizes and shapes, arrived at the meeting place early and discovered that the table behind which she was to stand had a drawer in it; so she placed the bottles in that drawer and only took out and put on the table those about which she was talking at the moment.

If large display charts are to be used, only a limited amount of material should be on each page and some type of rack should be provided so that only the page being discussed will be in sight.

Even such small matters as whether or not a pointer is needed should be thought of in advance.

Plan for variety

Variety is the spice which makes meetings palatable. The same old program in the same old way gets to be dull and uninteresting. Have your people come to the meetings with a feeling of expectancy and curiosity. For the introduction, and often for use in the meeting itself, plan something just a little different. In the shop, there can be an actual demonstration on a machine of how best to do a job, or all work spoiled in a month may be piled up on a table and the group asked to guess the cost. In the store, there can be a debate between two pieces of merchandise as to which can do the most for the customer (two salespeople representing the merchandise), or a "spelling-bee" type of contest in which the salespeople are divided into two groups to see which half has learned best the new fashion facts.

There are many such plans which can be used to make meetings more interesting and to warm people up to a point where they are ready to take a part in the discussion. Some of these things may be done on the spur of the moment when some happening makes them appropriate; but it is always well to have some such devices planned in advance. Then if inspiration fails there is always something to fall back on.

Location

Thought should be given to the place where the meeting is to be held. It should be so located that any passing through the meeting space will be behind the group. The light should be on the speaker rather than shining in the faces of the group. A little extra care in selecting the location can do much to make the meeting successful.

Notice

Everyone who is to attend should be notified of the meeting in ample time so that no other plans will be made, and all should be reminded of the meeting shortly before it is time to go to it.

Details

Many of these things may seem like mere details. They are details, but more often than not, the difference between success and failure in anything is one of attention to or lack of attention to details. Holding meetings is no exception. And so we shall discuss some more details, about the meeting itself.

The Meeting

On time

The meeting, especially if it is one of a series or a meeting held each week or month, should start on time. At first many may be late, but gradually those who attend regularly will learn to come on time.

The opening

There is probably no part of the program which should be more carefully planned than the first few sentences of your meeting. If the opening is dull and uninteresting, if it is apologetic, or if it is hesitant, you may lose your grip on your audience at the outset; and this is always difficult to recapture. Three methods have been tried over and over again, and are equally satisfactory. Plan to use one of the three. They are:

1. *Story*: A good story, well told, always makes an excellent opening, provided the story really fits into what is to follow and illustrates the point to be made. A story, no matter how good, which is entirely off the subject, or with only a vague connection, had better be left untold.

2. *Dialogue or playlet*: This is always good if short and clever; and, as in the case of the story, if it really illustrates the point.

3. *The "shock" question*: The asking of a definite question which you expect to answer later is perhaps the best opening of the three, especially if there are likely to be several answers, and the real point missed.

A store service executive wishes to reduce the number of wrong addresses:

"How much, on the average, do you think each package wrongly addressed costs us to handle before we finally get it to the customer?" Then after a few guesses and the correct answer. "But is this the most expensive part of a wrong address; what costs even more than this?" (After discussion the group will probably bring out that loss of customer good will is the most costly thing about wrong addresses.)

The shop foreman wants to get his men always to wear goggles when they grind their tools:

"How much in wages, money which might have been spent buying some things you and your families needed, do you think was lost in this department during the past year through lost time because of eye accidents?"

The Sunday-school teacher with a class of boys about thirteen years old would like to impress the fact that Jesus was a normal, everyday boy:

"Would Jesus play football if he were here today and going to school at Brown Junior High with you fellows?"

And so, for almost any subject, a question can be planned that, when the answer is developed by the group (not by the leader alone), will both create interest and point clearly to something the listeners should do about the subject being discussed.

Discussion

An effort should be made to get the members of the group to take active part in the discussion right from the outset.

Perhaps the most important single rule to be followed in the accomplishment of this is always to say, "Thank you, that's fine" or "That is an excellent thought, Mr. Jones," immediately after the first contribution from any member of the group. And you can say this sincerely and enthusiastically no matter how weak and halting that contribution may be, because you need this first contribution more than you need anything else. Without it your meeting may easily be a failure.

If you speak encouragingly, even flatteringly to this first contributor, you will find that others do not hesitate to venture their opinions; but the discussion leader who made the mistake of saying "No, that's wrong; I am afraid you misunderstood my question" found it most difficult to get things started again.

Even after the discussion is well under way the leader should rarely, if ever, contradict or even criticize a statement made by a member of the group. If it is incorrect the leader can ask for the opinion of the group and someone in the group will correct it. Criticism from the leader would tend to reduce participation.

If someone throws into the discussion a thought which is not on the subject being discussed some such answer as this may be used: "Thank you, Mr. Jones, that is an interesting suggestion, but we had better confine our discussion for the present to this one phase of the question. We shall not forget your suggestion, however, and if there is time we shall get to it a little later."

The person who is too shy to volunteer an opinion can usually be encouraged to take part by a direct question addressed to him. But make it an easy question, one he is sure to answer well. Often asking him to repeat some interesting comment which he made to you in private is an excellent way to encourage the shy person to take part. Be sure to thank him for the comment and refer to it occasionally by saying, "As Mr. Jones said, that matter can often be handled by," etc.

There are many other devices which the leader may use to provoke the thought necessary to good discussion. Some of these are: general or direct questions by the leader; questions assigned in advance; or the making of a statement by the leader which is not correct, then asking, "Is that true?"

"In answering discussion from the floor, it is always important to take a man at what he meant or would like to have said, rather than at what he actually said. Students, especially practical men, are often timid about talking publicly. Frequently in the embarrassment of speaking from the floor they say things in a way that if taken literally are quite different from what they intended.

"If the instructor differs with what they literally said when it is not what they meant, and publicly proves that what they said was wrong, they feel that they have been unfairly treated and say to themselves, 'If that's the way the class is going to be run, I'll shut up.'

"If, on the other hand, the teacher catches and adequately states the idea that a man was feeling his way toward, but was not able clearly to express, it gives the man a sense of elation and renewed self-confidence."[2]

Blackboard

Most leaders of discussion meetings have found it to their advantage to have a blackboard, and to write on the board the most important points as they are brought up. This is particularly valuable when using either the free discussion or case method, because in both of these the group itself builds a statement of fact and decides on methods of procedure and then the leader sums up at the end. Even though you as the leader undoubtedly have a good idea of the outline which will be developed, it is much more interesting to the group if this outline is actually developed on the blackboard. Also, the use of the blackboard keeps the eyes from wandering around the room and seeing other things which might be distracting.

Some group leaders, however, find the use of the blackboard itself to be distracting. This may be corrected by having some one other than the leader do the actual writing. Each should use his own judgment as to whether or not he wishes to use a blackboard.

Only rarely should a complete "outline" be put on the black-

[2] From *Psychology for Executives*, E. D. Smith (Harper & Brothers).

board in advance. This usually makes the meeting seem too cut and dried.

Encourage differences of opinion

Honest differences of opinion are highly desirable in a discussion group such as the usual business meeting. Without them the meetings will be somewhat flat and uninteresting. Skill in securing an honest expression of opinion, and in handling differences of opinion, is essential to success as a group leader. There are three main ways of settling differences of opinion:[3]

1. *Domination*, or the forcing of one person's opinion on another. Where the differences are intelligent and honest, such as they will usually be in a group discussing some business question, there is rarely a place for this method.

2. *Compromise*, which usually implies that each person, although not always fully convinced of the correctness or justice of it, gives up something so that a workable agreement can be reached.

3. *Integration*. No one really wants to be dominated by another or to compromise, because either settlement means a giving up of something. It is much better, if possible, to work out a solution in which both desires have found a place, so that neither side has had to sacrifice anything.

Let us take a simple illustration: In one of the smaller rooms of a library one day, Mr. Brown wanted the window open; Mr. Smith wanted it shut. Finally, they opened the window in the next room, where no one was sitting. This was not a compromise, because there was no curtailing of desire; both got what they really wanted. For Mr. Smith did not want a closed room; he simply did not want the north wind to blow directly on him; likewise, Mr. Brown did not want that particular window open; he merely wanted more air in the room.

This method of settling differences of opinion is called integration. The important thing for any leader of group discussion to remember is that the settling of differences of opinion by integration involves a broad understanding of the whole problem, an

[3] Adapted from part of a lecture on "Constructive Conflict," by Mary P. Follett, printed in *Scientific Foundations of Business Administration*, edited by H. C. Metcalf (Williams and Wilkins).

appreciation of what each contestant really wants (not just what he says), and a certain skill at invention, the finding of a solution which takes into account both viewpoints without sacrificing either.

One danger in the discussion method

One danger in any method which invites free discussion is that some one point of little importance may start a discussion which will take more time than that point justifies. To avoid this, you must always keep control and tactfully move the discussion along so that approximately the correct amount of time is given to each point.

Some meeting leaders prepare a time schedule and jot down in the margin of their notes how far they should be at each ten-minute period of the meeting. This is an excellent practice to follow, especially when the subject is one in which the discussion may easily take the form of a debate about some inconsequential point. Of course, such a schedule should not be followed too mechanically. If something really interesting and worth while comes up, the leader may decide to omit or postpone to a later meeting, part of what he had planned to present.

Keep your own enthusiasm at a high pitch

Unless you are enthusiastic about the importance of the subject and show that enthusiasm, you cannot expect the group to be enthusiastic.

One successful training director who has taught business subjects for many years sums up discussion so skillfully and announces with so much interest and enthusiasm the general principles and rules to which the discussion points that she gives to each person who has entered into the discussion the feeling that he has made a genuine contribution. Each principle is announced with all the enthusiasm she could possibly use if she were announcing a new discovery. She can do this, although she has announced the same principle many times before, because she knows that for some members of the group it is indeed a new discovery.

Close on time

Have a definite time limit. Plan to stop one or two minutes before the "dead line," and stick to your plan. A good meeting is somewhat hard to close, and there is a temptation to go on. It is always best to close your meeting with the group still hungry for more. They look forward then with pleasure to the next meeting.

The inspirational meeting

There is occasionally a meeting, such as a brief inspirational mass meeting, where discussion is not needed to make the meeting successful, but this is the exception rather than the rule.

After the Meeting

The follow-up after the meeting to see that the teaching has carried over into practice is as important as the actual teaching. It is easy to teach people to "know about"; but to teach them a completed learning process including capacity to do is more difficult. A few days after any meeting you have held which has had as its purpose getting people to do something, you should check by watching, by shopping, or by consulting records, to see if your people are doing the things you have taught. Then from time to time you should check again.

Persistent follow-up is necessary if teaching is to form permanently correct habits of action, and that is the real measure of the success of any teaching.

Suggested Supplementary Reading on Making Meetings Interesting

Influencing Human Behavior, H. A. Overstreet.

I. The Key Problem: Capturing the Attention; II. The Appeal to Wants; III. The Problem of Vividness; IV. The Psychology of Effective Speaking.

How To Train Supervisors, R. O. Beckman.

Part I is a manual of procedure containing chapters on: Objectives of Training, Group Discussion, The Method of Determinate Discussion, Stimulating Profitable Discussion, The Technique of Control, The Art of Making Up Wall Charts, Preparing to Present a Topic, The Evaluation of Results, and Steps in Organization and Administration.

Part II furnishes outlines for the discussion of thirty-two such subjects as: Responsibilities of the Supervisor or Foreman, Safety and Accident Prevention, Adapting Discipline to the Individual, How to Demonstrate a Job, Heading off Labor Trouble at its Source, and Leadership.

How to Be Interesting, Robert Emmons Rogers.
Especially Chapters I and II.

CHAPTER XII

Measuring and Rating Individual Performance

THE four terms most commonly applied to the measuring and rating of individual performance of employees are *performance rating*, *merit rating*, *employee appraisal* and *service rating*.

As applied in personnel administration, they are practically synonymous and any one of them might have been used in this chapter. The term "merit rating" was chosen, however, because it is the term that is probably most frequently used by business organizations that have formal rating plans.

Merit rating usually includes: (1) a carefully considered decision as to just what qualities of performance, aptitude, and attitude go together to make up the optimum person or job performance for each position, and what is the relative importance, or *weight*, of each of these qualities; (2) a careful and systematic rating of the degree to which each separate quality is shown in the person's job performance, prepared by a supervisor who has close personal contact with the work of the person being rated.

The supervisor should have before him *at the time he is actually preparing the rating* all available objective measures of the person's performance, including both *production factors* (sales, number of pieces made or processed, etc.) and *destruction factors* (spoilage, lost sales, errors, complaints, etc.). He should have, also, atendance records, records of suggestions made, and all other similar information. *And he should take all these into account and give proper weight to each of them as he makes his rating*. This making the fullest possible use of objective measures is so important that the rating form should be so designed as to make sure that it is done.

Merit rating may be defined, then, as an orderly, systematic, and carefully considered analysis and evaluation of a person's services, based on both observation over a considerable period of time and a study of all available objective records of performance and behavior.

IMPORTANCE OF MERIT RATINGS

The keynote of the whole program of personnel management of any organization should be a constant endeavor to achieve *fairness.* All rules and procedures should have as a major purpose an effort to ensure that all persons connected with the operation of the business are treated fairly and with consideration for their feelings.

The merit rating program, if properly planned and administered, aids in this endeavor in at least six important ways.

1. If carefully and objectively made, merit ratings form the fairest and best basis for decisions in considering salary increases, promotions, transfers, and layoffs.

True, merit ratings are not always fair, and the program does have in it possibilities for favoritism and injustice. *But it has also the possibility, with proper administration, of being made absolutely fair, while many salary plans, based as they so often are on only one or two parts of the whole desired job performance, are inherently unfair and often cannot be made otherwise even by conscientious and skillful administration.*

The difficulty of eliminating unfairness where compensation is based on production factors alone was forcefully brought home to me several years ago. Our wage-payment plan was a salary plus a monthly bonus based on how well sales quotas had been met. I gave out the bonus checks personally, so that I could talk with the salespeople about their whole performance—compliments or complaints of customers, errors made in cash-register or sales-check system, neatness and completeness of stock, etc.

After one of these distributions an operating executive made this remark:

"I have noticed, George, that the size of the checks you give out seems to be in inverse ratio to the general merit of the person, as might be judged by the nature of your comments to him. It seems to me to be about this way: You tell Miss Jones that she has a very bad record as to errors, that customers complain about her brusqueness, and that she really must keep her stock better—and you give her a check for $54.25. You compliment Miss Brown on the fact that there have been no errors in over six months and you show her two letters from customers commending her patience and helpfulness—and you give her a check for $1.78."

His comment was, of course, somewhat exaggerated—but not so much so as I should have liked to believe.

We revised our wage-payment plan.

2. The continuous observation of each phase of each employee's work efficiency and attitude and the making of notations and records necessary to an objective rating help the supervisor in his efforts to keep constantly alert to those things in the employee's work that need correction. Frequently he will be able to give the employee the needed help and guidance before the condition becomes serious, and the actual rating will be good.

3. The fact that once each year each employee is given a statement of just how his supervisors feel as to his general efficiency aids the employee greatly in his own efforts to do a really good job. It is not quite fair to expect the employee to measure up to a standard unless we tell him from time to time just how well we believe that he has done this—just how far along the road to achievement of the standard he has travelled.

4. The careful review and discussion of every phase of each employee's work which are necessary before each rating furnish an excellent preparation for an annual training interview at which the employee's entire record may be reviewed with him and suggestions for improvement given.

5. The careful review by higher executives of the ratings of all employees under their supervision minimizes the possibility of any employee with above-average qualifications being overlooked, even though he does not push himself forward.

6. The various activities incident to the design, installation, and administration of a merit rating program are important also as "springboards" to at least two other activities necessary to a well-rounded personnel program—one that endeavors to achieve a higher degree of fairness by inviting supervisors and employees to have a part in it.

Meetings of supervisors are a necessary part of the merit rating program. Their help is needed in reaching many decisions such as what qualities should be rated and what should be the weight given each; how the ratings should be used; whether employees should be told of their ratings, and, if so, how and by whom. The definitions used on the form must be discussed to ensure that all understand them alike. If skillfully handled, these meetings lead naturally and easily into the discussion of all types of problems in personnel supervision. And right there we have a program of training supervisors in this important subject under ideal conditions—free discussion, contributions made by all present, and problems solved together—rather than a formal "class" with someone acting as "teacher." Such meetings, conducted in just this manner, are vitally important in giving to the supervisors a fuller understanding of their part in making the personnel administration of the organization truly fair and considerate of the feelings of all.

Then there are the meetings of employees in small groups to discuss the plan, which are so important to their full understanding and acceptance of it. How the merit ratings may be made fully fair to the employee is a subject in which all employees are vitally interested and with respect to which they can be of real assistance to the management. Other questions on which the management wants and needs employee understanding and help can be skillfully introduced for discussion. And, without any fanfare of trumpets, a sound program of employee-employer participation in personnel management is started.

But Are Not Ratings Just "Personal Opinions"?[1]

"A long-standing criticism of rating is that it is subjective—after all, 'just a personal opinion.'

"It is true that individual ratings are frequently 'wrong' or 'unfair.' For example, the plant superintendent thinks that Supervisor Green is not interested in his job. As a matter of fact, Supervisor Green does extra work at home and slips down to the plant

[1] This excellent answer to the criticism that ratings are subjective and therefore of little value is quoted from "Rating of Supervisors," by Mary Harper Wortham, Bulletin #11 of the California Institute of Technology (Pasadena, Calif.).

on Sunday afternoons so that he can maintain what he feels is a calm and casual air during office hours. The plant superintendent, however, rates him low on interest, which we may say is a case of 'unfair rating.'

"People act on what they believe to be facts, and as far as the end result is concerned, mis-impressions might as well be facts. The plant superintendent did not make his error in judgment in regard to Green because of the rating form—the superintendent was in error in any case. Assuming that the superintendent's opinion is shared by Green's other superior officers who also rate him low on interest, the review of the rating with Green provides a much better chance that such an incorrect opinion may be revised than if such opinion had never been recorded and brought to Green's attention.

"Rating forms should not be condemned because of misjudgments which they record. To a certain extent the more errors there are, the greater the need for rating, because it provides the opportunity for correction: first, through the pooling of judgments of several raters; and second, through the review of the rating with the person rated."

Do We Need Merit Rating?

Every busines organization already has merit rating. Each time a supervisor recommends that an employee shall receive a salary increase or be promoted or each time a decision is made as to which of several employees in a department shall be laid off or furloughed, and that decision is based on an opinion as to the real merit of the employee, there has been a merit rating.

The question, then, is, rather, are we satisfied with our present merit rating program? Does it aid materially in our effort to ensure that all promotions, transfers, layoffs, and other personal actions are based on the actual merit of the employee? Are we being completely fair both to employee and to the management in the decisions we make? And are we fair to the supervisors when we ask them to make important recommendations without giving them all the assistance we can in the analysis of the facts underlying these recommendations?

Personnel decisions are important. They affect seriously the lives of people. Carelessly and unfairly made, they can tear down morale, cause attitudes to become antagonistic and embittered, lay the foundation for personal failure. Thoughtfully and fairly made and sympathetically administered, they build morale, find and correct those things which hold people back, and point the way to successful accomplishment.

It is important both from the viewpoint of the success of the business and from the viewpoint of service to society that personal decisions shall be made fairly.

A good merit rating program will not solve the whole problem; but it will help—and materially so.

Fundamental Requirements for a Successful Merit Rating Program

The program need not be elaborate or complicated. One of the most successful merit rating programs I have known was that used many years ago by the owner-manager of a shop of about five hundred employees. Twice each year he asked his foremen and department heads first to group the employees under their supervision by occupations—all lathe hands together, all salesmen together, etc.,—and then to arrange those listed under each occupation according to their general value to the firm—most valuable first, least valuable last.

After this was done, he sat down with each foreman and asked him just what had caused him to say that Bill was more valuable than Joe, etc. Also, he asked each foreman what he was doing to help those near the bottom of the list and gave suggestions for training or corrective measures. Those who stayed at or near the bottom of the list too long were usually laid off or furloughed during slack seasons, and those near the top usually received salary increases.

Probably as simple a program as this would not work so well in the more complex organizations of today as it did in this small shop; but it is interesting to note that, simple as the plan was, it satisfies at least five of the seven conditions usually considered necessary to success in merit rating. The only conditions not satisfied are that there shall be specific statements of standards and a rating form which has been thoughtfully and skillfully designed. It is quite likely that standards were discussed with the foremen and department heads. And it is just possible that the blank piece of paper used as a "rating form" in this plan, *with the clear and simple directions as to how to use it which were given*, was really more thoughtfully and skillfully designed than are some extremely complicated forms now in use.

The seven conditions that a study of many successful and unsuccessful rating programs seems to indicate as being necessary to full success are as follows:

1. *Top executives should be actively interested*

It is most important that the principal operating executives—the men who make the final decisions on promotions, salary increases, and layoffs—shall be fully "sold" on the value of the merit rating program and take an active part in its installation and operation.

2. *Supervisors should understand and approve the plan*

The most important condition of all to the success of any merit rating program is that the supervisors shall understand the plan fully, have faith in its effectiveness, and carry out their part conscientiously.

The original rating is made by the employee's immediate supervisor. If this rating is made carelessly or unintelligently, no amount or care and intelligence elsewhere will save the program. It is a failure at the beginning.

3. *A rating form that has been thoughtfully and skillfully designed should be used*

A well-designed form is of great help in securing the accuracy and uniformity so important in any rating program, especially when ratings of different supervisors must be compared with each other. Such a form should meet the following seven standards, all of which will be discussed in fuller detail later:

First, the list of qualities on which ratings are to be asked should be so selected that every quality is important to the optimum job performance but there are no qualities included which are not important.

Second, the list of qualities should be so selected that the total job performance is divided into enough distinct parts to facilitate analysis to determine the reasons for any unsatisfactory performance but not into so many parts that there is confusion. Not less than five or more than ten qualities is the usual practice.

Third, there should be included in this list qualities that have to do with the person's *attitude* as well as with his *aptitude* and *production.* An employee, especially one whose duties involve very little contact with the public, can probably turn out a good volume of satisfactory work even though his attitude toward supervision, his willingnes to cooperate with employees around him, and his loyalty to the business as a whole leave much to be desired; but it is highly probable that this attitude will cause others, both the supervisor and fellow employees, occasionally to become so upset that they cannot do their best work. This employee "spoils work" as surely as if he were careless about how he operated his lathe or his bookkeeping machine.

Fourth, to each quality there should be assigned a value, or *weight*, so that the total numerical score will represent, with reasonable accuracy, the total merit of the person's job performance. Even relatively small differences in numerical scores should represent like differences in job performance.

Fifth, definitions and instructions should be so worded that, as nearly as possible, they will be understood alike by all who read them. Such everyday words as "satisfactory" and "good" when used in definitions seem to be especially confusing. To one young supervisor, a recent graduate of a strict military school, nothing much short of perfection was satisfactory. To another, work just good enough to get by without serious censure was considered good enough to be so graded.

Sixth, in planning the wording of definitions and instructions, thought should also be given to the probable effect on employee morale. Employees will and should see the rating forms and know exactly how they have been rated. Even a low general rating and definitions at the lower end of the scale can be so worded that they will create a desire to do better, rather than merely engender antagonism because of their brusqueness.

Seventh, there should be included in the design of the form itself devices that minimize or, at least, detect carelessness or lack of understanding of meanings and that tend to increase the objectiveness of the ratings.

4. *Clear, specific, detailed directions should be used*

The ideal of any rating plan is for a score of 75 given by one supervisor to one employee to mean exactly the same as a measure of general value to the organization as does a score of 75 given by a different supervisor to another employee doing the same type of work. This ideal can never be completely realized; but efforts toward that goal will be aided greatly if each supervisor uses exactly the same technique of rating as do all other supervisors.

This can be accomplished only when there are clear, specific, and detailed directions as to just how the rating is to be carried out. And the supervisors themselves should play an important part in writing these directions.

5. *There should be standards to aid in forming judgments*

An important part of any merit rating plan which attempts to review and rate performance, is a statement of standards of performance—standards which will enable both the employee and the rater to have some basis for judgment as to how satisfactory the employee's performance has been. These standards should be stated in as specific terms as is possible.

6. *Thorough and continued training for raters is essential*

Training at the time the system is installed can best be accomplished by asking the supervisors to help in designing and installing the plan. Then immediately after each rating all supervisors should be asked to make any suggestions that occur to them for improvements in the form or administration. The personnel director should also make note of any questions that have been asked him and informal suggestions that have been made to him. *Shortly before the next rating, all* these suggestions and questions should be discussed at meetings of supervisors, and any suggested changes voted on.

7. *Ratings should be used skillfully and sympathetically in training and correction*

Perhaps the primary purpose of most merit rating programs

is *employee appraisal*, to be used as a basis for setting salaries, deciding on promotions, and making other important personnel decisions. But only a part of the possible value of the rating program is realized if this is the only use made of the information on the rating forms.

A Typical Merit Rating Form

The form shown on pages 143 and 144 has been used for several years in the Farm Credit Administration of Columbia and has proven most satisfactory for all types of nonsupervisory employees.

The rating manual which is given to supervisors who use the form contains the following definitions of the qualities rated:

Quality of Work

The rating on this quality will indicate the supervisor's opinion as to the average degree of excellence of the work this employee has done for the entire period being rated; but *it will not take into account the volume of work done.*

It will take into account all such factors as neatness, accuracy, completeness and general acceptability of the work done.

It will take into account also *the importance of each factor*. For example, errors on work which goes out without further checking are most serious. Therefore, accuracy would be given a higher "weight" in rating "quality of work" where this is true than it would on work which is regularly checked.

In field positions, such factors as thoroughness in securing information, judgment in making recommendations, and ingenuity and resourcefulness in working out solutions for difficult servicing problems would all be rated under "quality of work."

In any type of work an occasional thoughtless oversight or error would, of course, cause "quality of work" to be rated lower than would be the case if such mistakes were not made, but care should be exercised not to give too much weight to one or two recent mistakes when the total number for the entire period being rated is small.

Volume of work

When rating this quality, both how rapidly the person works

Form P-10—Revised 4-42.

EMPLOYEE APPRAISAL

Employee's Name__________ Classification __________

Bank ______ Dept.______ Div.______ Section ______

Unit __________ Rating Supervisor__________

This form is designed to help you to appraise accurately the value of your employees to the organization. You are asked to rate the employee on each of several traits or qualities listed here.

After each trait there is a line representing various degrees of the trait. Each of the phrases under the lines describes the amount or degree of that trait represented by the point directly over the phrase. You rate any employee by putting your check mark at the place on the line which represents your judgment as to his possession of the trait. If the true description would fall between two of the descriptions given, you should put your check between the two, nearer the one which is nearer the correct description.

In view of the importance of this rating, both to the employee and to the organization, you are urged to study and observe carefully the suggestions furnished you with these forms

QUALITY OF WORK	15	16.5	18	19.5	21	22.5	24	25.5	27	28.5	30
	Quality is unsatisfactory.		Quality is often not quite up to average of general run of comparable employees.		Quality is about average of general run of comparable employees.		Quality of work is superior to that of general run of comparable employees.		Exceptionally high quality.		

Comment:

VOLUME OF WORK	15	16.5	18	19.5	21	22.5	24	25.5	27	28.5	30
	Very slow.		Inclined to be somewhat slow.		Output is about average of general run of comparable employees.		Turns out more work than general run of comparable employees.		Exceptionally high output.		

Comment:

KNOWLEDGE OF WORK	5	5.5	6	6.5	7	7.5	8	8.5	9	9.5	10
	Very little knowledge of his work.		Insufficient knowledge of some phases of the job.		Reasonably adequate knowledge of the job.		Excellent knowledge of his work.		Has exceptional knowledge of all phases of his work.		

Comment:

INITIATIVE	5	5.5	6	6.5	7	7.5	8	8.5	9	9.5	10
	A routine worker; usually waits to be told.		Often waits unnecessarily for directions.		Does regular work without waiting for directions.		Resourceful; alert to opportunities for improvement of work.		Seeks and sets for himself additional tasks; highly self-reliant.		

Comment:

WORK ATTITUDE	5	5.5	6	6.5	7	7.5	8	8.5	9	9.5	10
	Goes about his work half-heartedly.		Sometimes appears indifferent.		Shows normal, average interest in work.		Shows great interest in work.		Exceptionally enthusiastic about his work.		

Comment:

ATTITUDE TOWARD OTHERS	5	5.5	6	6.5	7	7.5	8	8.5	9	9.5	10
	Inclined to be quarrelsome, surly, touchy or uncooperative; upsets morale.		Sometimes difficult to work with.		About average in tactfulness and cooperation.		Always congenial and cooperative.		An unusual and strong force for office morale.		

Comment:

TOTAL SCORE________

and how consistently he maintains that speed should be considered. It is the total volume over the full period of time being rated which counts, not the rate made in sudden bursts of speed. For example, a typist who has the ability, as shown by the test, to type over 80 net words a minute might work so intermittently

GENERAL RATING: Considering all of the qualities you have rated on the reverse side of this form and any other qualities the employee may possess which affect his general value to the organization, please check the statement below which best describes him. Remember that the comparison is with all other persons you have ever known doing work of this type and class and not with just the other employees in the group under your supervision.

A. An exceptional employee; one of the best in his type and class of work I have ever known........ ☐

B. Stands out clearly as superior to the general run of employees doing work of the same general type and class........ ☐

C. A good employee; well fitted to his work, but not outstanding........ ☐

D. A fairly good employee, but somewhat less efficient than the general run of employees doing work of the same general type and class........ ☐

E. Serious weaknesses in work efficiency or attitude, or both, make it doubtful whether he will be satisfactory in the work he is doing........ ☐

F. I believe this employee to be definitely unsuited to the work he is doing, and probably unsuited to any work in the division in which he now works........ ☐

PLEASE INDICATE BY CHECK MARK HOW PROMISING AS PROMOTIONAL MATERIAL YOU BELIEVE THIS EMPLOYEE TO BE:

Future growth doubtful	Only moderate development ahead	Shows fair promise.	Very promising promotional material.	Great future growth probable; should go far.

COMMENTS:

GENERAL COMMENTS BY RATING SUPERVISOR:

RATING AND COMMENTS MADE BY:........ ....
Date

COMMENTS BY REVIEWING RATER:

BY:........ ....
Date

that the total volume for a week or month would be less than that of a person with a much lower test score.

The quality of the work done should not be taken into account in this rating. Thus a machine tool operator who turns out a large number of pieces should be rated high even though his spoilage is excessive. He would, of course, be rated low in "quality of work."

Knowledge of work

The rating on this quality should be on the basis of how completely the employee is in possession of all information about all types of work he will be called upon to do in performing the duties of his position. A clerk doing routine work would, of course, not need as extensive knowledge to secure a high rating as would a person who, in the regular course of his duties, might be called upon for recommendations as to changes in procedures or policies. But to secure a rating of "excellent," any one doing even routine work should, in addition to a knowledge of all essential rules and procedures, have at least a *fair* understanding of the basic principles behind the rules and procedures. To secure a rating of "exceptional" he should have an exceptional knowledge of rules and procedures plus a good understanding of underlying principles.

Here, however, as in the rating on all qualities, the decision is to be made on the basis of comparison with all other persons the supervisor has known doing this general type and class of work rather than with theoretical perfection. Thus, if the knowledge possessed by the person being rated would rank him in the top one or two per cent of all the people the supervisor has ever known doing this general type and class of work he would put his check mark at or near the extreme right of the scale even though he might consider the employee's knowledge considerably below theoretical perfection.

Initiative

Initiative is the capacity for assuming responsibility and starting and doing things without waiting for detailed instructions as to how to handle each step. It requires the ability to make promptly the decision as to what is the best course and the self-confidence and courage to act on that decision. A person with initiative will be on the alert for better methods of doing his work and will volunteer suggestions for changes rather than to wait until he is asked.

In rating this quality too much weight should not be put on the *judgment* used. This is primarily a rating of initiative. If an employee shows active initiative, but occasionally makes errors in judgment, there should, along with his high rating in initiative, be some such comment as: "Interested and shows considerable initiative but, probably due to lack of experience, is occasionally lacking in judgment." This lack of judgment would, of course, also be reflected in a lowered rating in "quality of work," *but not in the rating on initiative.*

Work attitude

How much interested is this person in his work? When emergencies arise and more than the usual effort is necessary, does he jump into the task with enthusiasm, or does he need to be reminded several times that his work is getting behind? Does he seem anxious to learn more about his work? Is he on the alert for new ideas? Is he taking some course or reading books which will help him to do a better job?

All, or practically all, of these questions must be answerable strongly in the affirmative before a high rating on "work attitude" can be given.

And care should be exercised not to judge solely by how much the person talks about being interested. There are employees who are not at all demonstrative, but who are genuinely interested and enthusiastic about their work and whose work attitude may be even better than that of those who talk more. Enthusiasm should be judged by what the employee does more than by what he says; by how he works more than by how he talks.

Attitude toward others

How pleasantly does this employee work with fellow employees? What is his attitude toward supervision? Does he welcome or does he resent suggestions made by his supervisors? When he is asked to do something a little out of the ordinary, how promptly and how pleasantly does he agree to do it? If he comes into contact with persons from outside the organization, are these contacts such that they build good will for the organization? Especially if he works directly with customers, does he show a sincere interest in them and their problems? All of these questions should be considered when rating this important quality.

The ratings on the first two qualities (quality of work and volume of work) make an overall rating on the work performance of the employee and, as such, are given much higher "weights" in computing the total score than are the other qualities. (The small numbers on the rating form indicate the numerical values or "weights" given the various ratings.)

The first two ratings have to do with the work more than with the person, the remaining four have to do with the person more than with the work.

There will be a certain overlapping as, for example, when some personal quality, such as initiative, enables the person to turn out more work or better work (or both). This quality would in this way affect two, or possibly three, ratings. This is desirable as it automatically increases the weight given to any personal quality which has an important bearing on work performance; but gives a relatively low weight to any personal quality which, while desirable, is not of major importance for success on the job.

The "Total Score" is obtained by adding the numerical values of the ratings on the separate qualities.

Some Other Types of Merit Rating

Rating by the Ranking Method

Many careful students of merit rating believe that a more valid rating is obtained when each employee is compared with another employee doing a similar type of work rather than when each employee's performance is compared with a "standard of performance." This type of rating is frequently accomplished by selecting first the best all-around employee, then the poorest, then the best employee remaining, then the poorest remaining, and so on.

The Check-List Type of Rating Form

An interesting variation of the usual type of rating form is one on which there are fifty or more favorable statements about work performance in the type of work in which the employee is being rated and about related qualities such as initiative and co-operation. A few such statements follow:

1. Turns out a large amount of work.
2. Is safety-minded.
3. Is very open-minded.
4. Understands his own work thoroughly.
5. Is a good team worker.

The supervisor, when making the rating, checks only the items which apply. The more items checked (since all are favorable), the higher the score.

The "Forced-Choice" Type of Rating Form

A recent development in merit rating technique is the forced-choice method. The rating form is made up of several groups of relatively unrelated statements. One such group follows:

— Has mechanical sense.
— Very serious-minded person.
— Has capacity for better work.
— Looks like a "comer."
— His profanity creates a very unfavorable impression.

The rater must choose which of the five statements in each group he believes to be the *most* descriptive and which the *least* descriptive of the person being rated. In other words he is "forced" to make two choices from each group of statements—hence the designation "forced-choice" method.

The key for scoring is confidential, so the rater does not know whether his choices of statements are, on the whole, favorable or unfavorable to the person being rated.

A serious drawback to a wider use of this type of rating is that the construction of the rating form and scoring key requires great skill and technical knowledge and a considerable expenditure of time in research. This method of rating should not be undertaken except with the guidance of a competent industrial psychologist.

Discussing the Rating With the Employee

An important, perhaps the most important, part of the merit rating program is the discussion of the rating with the employee. Most employees *want* to do good work, and most employees *can* do good work if they have standards by which to measure their performance and are shown in just what places they are not measuring up to the standards.

Much depends, of course, on how the supervisor goes about the task of telling the employee the results of the rating. Suggestions on how best to help the employee do better work are given in other chapters in this book, especially in Chapters XIII and XIV.

Suggested Supplementary Reading on Merit Rating

Rating Employee and Supervisory Performance, Dooher and Marquis (American Management Association).

This manual is made up of a selection of the best material AMA has published on the subject and, in addition, a specially prepared section based on AMA research.

Handbook of Personnel Management, George D. Halsey.

Chapter XIII, Employee Merit Rating.

Measuring and Rating the Worker, John B. Probst.

An excellent description of the check-list plan of rating, which was originated by the author.

CHAPTER XIII

Correcting Without Offending

CORRECTION is not the most pleasant task the supervisor is called upon to perform; but in that task lies his greatest opportunity for real service to people. Skillfully and sympathetically done, correction builds character, restores courage and self-confidence, and increases rather than destroys happiness.

The supervisor who merely hands out work to the people in his department, prodding them now and then for more production, "firing" those whose work fails to come up to the standard, hiring others and "firing" them if they do not make good—that supervisor makes no worth-while contribution to his firm, to the people under his supervision, or to society. He has improved no one. His only contribution to society is a bad one in that he has added to any feeling of bitterness, fear, hate, and failure which may already have existed.

But the supervisor who, when he finds people in his department whose work is not as it should be, looks for and discovers ways to help them to correct the faults which are holding them back, and patiently and skillfully leads them out of failure into success—that supervisor has made a real contribution to his firm, to the people under his supervision, and to society. Correction, real correction, is the finest act of supervision. It corrects faulty performance by searching for and correcting the causes rather than by browbeating and threatening. It builds self-confidence and courage rather than fear, and enthusiastic cooperation rather than unwilling compliance.

The technique of correction has ten "commandments."

The Ten Commandments of Correction

1. *Try first to get all pertinent facts*

Too often we leap into an attempt at correction with an inadequate knowledge of the facts. When we do this, we usually limp out of the interview having accomplished little but to antagonize the person corrected.

Frequently, when we do obtain the facts, we find that what we had thought to be a case which needed discipline was really the result of poor teaching or poor placement on our own part and, if anyone needed a reprimand, we were that person. So the first question should always be "Have I done my part?"

Then there should be careful checking of other circumstances which might have caused the poor work. A clerk in the accounting department makes frequent errors. His job is gathering information from several sources, and preparing reports. Much of his information comes from carbon copies which, while reasonably clear, are sometimes difficult to read. One of the first questions which should be asked, even before the man's faults are brought to his attention is, does he have adequate light? If a check shows six to eight foot candles—and all too often this will be the case—step this up to 20- or 25-foot candles, and note the reduction of errors.

It is surprising how much correction can be accomplished by an improvement in lighting alone. If you have a department in which the employees do close work, and you notice a serious tendency in them to leave their desks frequently, to go to the wash room for a smoke, to go to the files unnecessarily, to go across the street to the soda fountain—check the lighting. If you find it inadequate, according to a table which any lighting company will furnish, step up the illumination without saying a word to anyone. Check conditions again in two weeks, and you will often be surprised by the improvement.

Next to poor light, probably the greatest cause of inefficiency and bad dispositions on the part of employees who work seated at a desk or bench is poor seating equipment. Many firms save money in chairs, and spend it many times over in the payroll. Employees often are "bawled out" for poor work due largely if not entirely to faulty equipment or tools.

The primary requisite for successful correction is fairness; that no one shall be blamed for that which is not his fault.

If, after having all available facts, it is decided that a corrective interview is necessary, there are definite rules to be followed if this interview is to accomplish its purpose, that of making the correction and leaving the person with self-confidence and enthusiasm unimpaired.

In no phase of personnel supervision has a more definite step-by-step technique been worked out, and in no phase is it more essential to success that all of the "commandments" be obeyed.

2. *If possible, choose a place which is both private and quiet*

Correction should never be made in the presence of another employee, except such brief correction as may be necessary to stop, while it is being done, something which may cause injury to a person or damage to property. For instance, a stock boy dragging a dress along the floor or a tool boy carelessly tapping a casting with the edge of a cutting tool should be corrected, even though someone else is present. Any further discussion of the matter and any caution that such careless behavior must be stopped should, however, be in private. The place and time should be carefully chosen, so that there will be no interruptions.

Reasonable quiet also is important. If the interviewer and the person being corrected have to raise their voices to drown out other noise, there is a tendency in both to become excited.

3. *Always begin with a question*

There is probably no one rule in personnel supervision which is more absolute than the rule that every corrective interview should be begun with a question. In my own experience of over thirty-five years, I can remember no exception.

Even in cases where we feel absolutely sure that a severe reprimand is justified we lose nothing by opening with a question, and we may save ourselves embarrassment. Even when we feel absolutely sure, we are sometimes mistaken. We may feel, for example, that there can be no question about the guilt of a tool boy caught using a micrometer as a nutcracker, and that we shall be fully justified in starting the "corrective interview" in about the following manner:

"You —— ——— blockhead, quit using that 'mike' for a nutcracker."

But the answer may be:

"I'm not so dumb as you think. This 'mike' is no good. It is an old one all sprung out of shape; the tool room foreman gave it to me to take home for my kid brother to play with. But it makes a swell nutcracker. Want to try it?"

Where then is our dignity, poise, prestige?

But if we begin with the question, "Why are you using a 'mike' to crack nuts?" we can answer the boy's explanation and invitation to try his new nutcracker with the comment, "No, thank you, but that is a new one on me," and make our exit, dignity unimpaired.

On the other hand, if the boy's answer reveals that he is using a good "mike" as a nutcracker, we can then quickly reach a decision as to whether he is ignorant or careless, and can go ahead either with instruction or reprimand, as the case demands.

May I illustrate further with an actual example from my own experience? There was a vacancy in one of our furniture departments. Mr. Bowen had been the proprietor of a small country store, but had failed in business, and was in desperate need of work. Although his experience was limited, he had such a pleasing personality and seemed so much in earnest about needing a job and being willing to work hard to learn that the buyer and I decided to give him a chance.

He came to work on Monday. Wednesday he was half hour late. Thursday he was late again, and Friday did not come in at all. He was on time Saturday and Monday, but did not seem to show much interest in his work. His mind was somewhere else. Tuesday he was two hours late. Tuesday afternoon I sent for him. My patience was about gone. I felt that I had recommended him for the job partly because of sympathy and the belief that he had "thrown me down" so badly was the thought uppermost in my mind. So I must admit that he had scarcely seated himself in my office before I "lit into him" for his complete failure to keep his promises. It was some seconds before he could interrupt to say, "But, Mr. Halsey, didn't the assistant buyer tell you the reason?"

Then he told me his story. He had brought his wife and two

small children down from the country to a small apartment in town the Saturday before he began work. They were scarcely settled when his older girl ran a temperature, and on Tuesday, the day I sent for him, she had to be taken to the hospital with what they thought was double mastoid infection. The other child was sick in bed, also, and, to add to it all, his wife was taken sick.

You can imagine how I felt. I apologized as best I could, and immediately sent our nurse to his apartment and the hospital to see what could be done. We arranged with one of the best surgeons in the city to operate without cost. The illnesses of the wife and younger child proved not to be serious, and with the aid of a visiting nurse and our nurse they were soon up and around. It was not long before the older child, too, was on the road to recovery. Mr. Bowen later proved to be one of the best men in the department.

How much better it would have been had I started:

"Mr. Bowen, I notice you have been late several times in the past week, and I sent for you to ask you the cause, and to see if we can help you correct it."

Or, even better, if I had gone to the department and inquired a little and found out the cause myself, *before* I sent for Mr. Bowen.

This happened years ago, but it made such an impression on me that I do not think I have, since that day, ever begun the actual corrective part of any interview with anything but a question. It is a good practice to follow. It may save embarrassment for you and enable you to do a better job of correction.

But be careful to avoid the mistake Bill Towne made. He had attended a series of meetings in which the importance of beginning each corrective interview with a question had been discussed at some length, so at the first opportunity he decided to apply the rule.

In his department there was a man, Tom Ashley, who was an excellent workman with long experience in performing a difficult operation necessary in the assembly of one of the machines manufactured by the company. But, recently, Tom had been absent quite frequently and often when he came in he looked somewhat "bleary-eyed" as if he had been drinking the night before.

So Bill decided to talk to Tom. He called him over to his desk, which was in a quiet corner of the department where no one could hear what was said. And he opened the interview with a question:

"Tom, why are you getting drunk almost every night and letting me down on the job the way you are? You know we are behind on our deliveries of Model 27, and that you are my best man on that model. Why don't you let drink alone and come to work every day?"

Tom explained to Bill, in none too friendly a manner, that he had not been drinking at all, but that his absence had been caused by the serious illness of his wife, that when he appeared on the job "bleary-eyed" the cause was loss of sleep; that he had not for years touched anything stronger to drink than black coffee. And later investigation proved all these statements to be true.

Tom was a quiet sort of a fellow and didn't often lose his temper, but he did lose it that day. He told Bill just what he thought of him and then said he was going to the office for his time because he was through.

Bill succeeded in persuading Tom to stay, and as his wife's health improved his attendance became normal again.

At the next supervisors' meeting Bill told of his experience, and the group decided to add this to the rule:

Always begin with a question but be sure that the question is not so worded that it is, itself, an accusation.

They decided that it would have been much better had Bill opened his interview in some such manner as this:

"Tom, you have been absent quite a little lately, what's the trouble? Is there anything causing your absence we can help you with?"

4. *Give the person being corrected ample opportunity to talk*

Possibly the employee has a real reason (or at least thinks he has) for his action, and if he gets a chance to tell this you can more easily find a way to help him. He may wander away from the immediate subject, but such wanderings are often more revealing of the real cause of the difficulty than would be the answers to specific questions. Do not hurry the interview. Listen attentively.

Interrupt only to ask some question now and then concerning

significant details or to point out tactfully some fact of which the employee may not be aware.

It is not necessary that you agree but if you do disagree, do so without argument. Some such comment as "I don't really believe that Tom has it in for you as you say, but I am interested to know just why you think so, so I can help straighten out matters" is not antagonizing nor does it put you in the position of agreeing when you do not feel that you should agree.

5. *Consider carefully all of the evidence*

You have, before the interview, gathered all the information you could. You have, in the interview, heard the employee's side of the question and have tried to look at it in the light of his opinions and feelings. You are now in position to decide what you believe to have been the real cause of the error or difficulty. When this is done the hardest part of the task of correction is completed; decision as to the nature and extent of correction necessary is relatively easy.

It may be that the new evidence will cause you to decide that no correction at all is necessary. If so, you should close the interview promptly and pleasantly. If you have begun the interview with the right kind of a question the employee need never know that correction was in your mind, and nothing will have been taken away from his interest in his work, his self-confidence, and his feeling that he is being treated fairly.

6. *Fit the method of correction to the individual*

Many supervisors use exactly the same approach for every individual. This is poor technique. One person may be sensitive, and a blunt approach may merely antagonize and hurt him, making impossible any real teaching. And this, after all, is the real purpose of the corrective interview.

For another person a blunt, straight-from-the-shoulder statement of his fault and what he must do to correct it may be necessary to get results, although this is not frequently true.

Ability and willingness on the part of a supervisor to adapt himself to others, rather than to expect others always to adapt themselves to him, is an important qualification for success in supervision, even when the supervisor is handling a problem in discipline—possibly even more so then than at other times.

There is one important point to be kept constantly in mind and it is that *the purpose of correction is to correct;* to make sure that whatever there is which is not as it should be will be eliminated. Punishment is definitely not the purpose, although some disciplinary action may at times be necessary.

The securing of a positive admission from the employee that he is wrong and is sorry is not necessary, if the supervisor feels that the employee has admitted this *to himself* and will discontinue the undesirable behavior.

The purpose of correction is to correct, nothing else.

7. *Maintain your own calmness regardless of the employee's attitude*

It is important that the interview be kept on as impersonal a basis as possible. The moment an executive lets the corrective interview descend to the plane of argument it has lost its effectiveness. The less any executive thinks or says about his power, his dignity, his feelings, his prerogatives, and the more he thinks and says about job standards, the more successful will be the interview.

The person interviewed may even make some uncomplimentary remarks concerning you, and in this case it will be difficult to eliminate personal feelings. You should always, however, endeavor to think only in terms of job requirements and how the person has fallen short in meeting these requirements, rather than of any affront to your own feelings.

8. *Close pleasantly; restore self-confidence*

When the person has indicated what you believe to be a sincere desire to correct his fault, and the necessary directions as to how to go about it have been given, the interview should be closed.

In the course of the interview, however, it may have been necessary to point out clearly to the person just where he is falling short of what his job requires. It may even be necessary to point out that he just cannot expect to continue to hold his job unless he shows marked improvement. If such unpleasant facts must be told, there should be no hesitation or equivocation about telling them. All of this, however, will leave the employee somewhat low in spirits. If the interview is closed with the employee feeling this way, he will go back to the job in anything but the proper frame of mind for success.

His courage and self-confidence must be restored and his enthusiasm renewed. It is well, then, to close the interview by mentioning his good qualities, and assuring him that you are certain that he will have no difficulty in eliminating the one thing which is holding him back, if he will really try. Offer to help in any way you can, and invite him to come back to see you at any time to discuss his progress.

In some cases, where the employee really has the ability, but is failing primarily because he is not taking his job seriously enough, a definite warning may be given that the employee must do better work or you must dismiss him. Even in a case like this the interview should close pleasantly with a statement on your part that you do have confidence in the employee's ability.

In any case, the employee should leave with the definite feeling that there is nothing personal about the whole thing. Many successful executives make it a point, after a corrective interview, to find some opportunity during the day to stop at the employee's desk or machine and make some brief comment, possibly complimenting or asking a friendly question about some work he is doing. This is effective in removing any feeling that there is a personal grudge.

9. *Follow up with a second interview, if necessary*

After any corrective interview, the employee's performance should be watched closely, but unobtrusively. If this watch indicates a completely corrected condition, you should try to forget the whole matter and not bring it up again in further conversation. But if observation shows sulkiness, depression, bitterness or refusal to correct bad habits, there must be a further interview.

After a reasonable, but not too long a time, if the correction has not proven fully effective the employee should be sent for again. A good opening sentence might be: "I just sent for you to ask you if there were any points about our talk last week which were not clear. As I remember it, you said that you were going to," etc.

This approach, which brings in the thought that the person

may have misunderstood the first interview, allows him, even at this late date, to correct his wrong attitude without sacrificing his dignity.

If the second interview fails to bring results, it will probably be wise for you to ask the advice of your superior as to what may be another method of approach. Occasionally, but not often, it is wise to send the person directly to a higher executive, so that executive may see what he can do to correct a serious fault.

10. *Do not use correction too often*

Do not let correction descend to the level of nagging. It is a wise supervisor who knows when to correct and when to overlook certain incorrect procedures.

Sometimes, when a person is trying hard and yet slips a little, it may be wise for the time not to call his attention to these slips. It is possible that he is trying to overcome them himself and will do so if a reasonable time is given. You should, however, not wait too long, because incorrect methods, if allowed to continue, have a way of becoming habits which are hard to break.

Suggested Supplementary Reading on Correction

Personal Leadership in Industry, Craig and Charters.
Chapter XI, The Reprimand. "Properly used, the reprimand is the most important single device of leadership and supervision."

Human Nature at Work, Jean L. Shepard.
Chapter VI, On the Job: Criticism (pp. 103–118).

Constructive Discipline in Industry, American Management Association.
This is a special research report in which fifty-eight business organizations co-operated.

CHAPTER XIV

The Supervisor's Problem Cases

The Correct Attitude

In the experience of everyone responsible for guiding and supervising the efforts of others there will be cases in which usual methods do not bring expected results—cases of people who do not seem to be able to adjust themselves properly to either the job or the group with which they work, and who are constantly causing trouble, themselves complaining or being complained about by other employees. Often, however, such people have unusual capacity to do good work, were it not for some peculiar viewpoints. An executive with long experience once remarked that it was surprising how often the people who had in one way or another been his "problem cases" turned out to be his best people, and, in many instances, had become successful executives themselves.

A supervisor's success or failure in the handling of these "problem people" will depend, more than on any other one thing, on the attitude he takes toward them, their grievances and their complaints.

First of all, there must be a real interest in the employee's problem and a genuine desire to settle the complaint to the employee's full satisfaction if this is at all possible.

There must, also, be a feeling of gratitude for the opportunity given to correct a cause of dissatisfaction rather than resentment or annoyance because of the complaint; and this feeling must be made evident by the supervisor's manner.

Finally, there must be *a full appreciation of the fact that the employee may be sincere in the belief that he is right, even though it is obvious to any unbiased observer that he is wrong.*

This attitude must be sincere. The executive who still retains in the back of his mind some idea of leadership as the exercise of power and dominion over others, will not be successful in eliminating the causes of dissatisfaction. The most he can do will be to suppress for a time the outward manifestations of dissatisfaction.

Disappointments and Personality

The exact manner in which we have met disappointments throughout our lives has probably had more to do with molding our personalities than has any other one thing, often having an effect on our attitudes and behavior long after the actual disappointments have been almost entirely forgotten. This is brought about by the effect these disappointments have had on that important something we call the ego.

"Ego" may be defined as the sum total of all that a person thinks of himself, good and bad; especially how he inwardly rates himself as compared with others of his group on things which he considers important or worth while. One's ego is constantly rising and falling as each experience contributes its part. No stock on the market has more frequent or more violent ups and downs. It expands and rises with attention, any opportunity for self-expression, praise, honors, affection, the enjoyment of new ventures, or success in any competition. This is especially true when there are others present to witness and applaud the success. But it shrinks and falls with inattention, domination by others, criticism, embarrassment, disgrace, or failure in competition. We all enjoy intensely its rise, and are cut deeply by those experiences which cause it to fall.

In fact, we enjoy so much and protect so ardently any feeling of personal worth-whileness or importance which we may have, be it little or much, that the doing of anything which will cause us to "lose face" and thus lower this sense of importance will be avoided at almost any cost. It will often be avoided unreasoningly, even violently, if less drastic methods are not effective.

Disappointments will come to all of us, however, no matter how hard we try to avoid them. The more these disappointments take away from our egos the more keenly they will be felt. Sometimes the hurt may be so great that we must find some way, not always a healthful way, to alleviate the pain. Any long continued sense of personal inferiority or feeling of shame seems to be unendurable. That all-important feeling of personal worth-whileness must be restored. If this is not done in a normal, fact-facing, healthful manner, it will be done in some less desirable way. *It must be done.*

Most examples of peculiar or abnormal behavior are the result of unhealthful or socially unacceptable ways in which the individual is trying, successfully or otherwise, to protect his ego—to keep his sense of personal worth-whileness from being impaired or to restore it if it has been impaired.

Whenever one finds that for some reason he has been stopped from doing something he had wanted most strongly to do or when he has made a failure of what he had hoped would be a triumph, there are two ways in which he can meet the situation.

1. He may endeavor to find the true facts and, facing these facts squarely, work out a solution which takes them fully into account.

2. He may refuse to face the facts and endeavor to escape reality by working out some solution based on only part of the facts or on pure fictions which are more pleasant than the facts.

When a man does have the courage to examine fairly and impersonally the facts in a situation in which he has met with serious disappointment, he will, as a rule, reach the conclusion that part at least of the disappointment was his own fault and could have been avoided had he acted differently.

This done, there are at least three satisfactory and emotionally healthful ways in which he may remedy the situation and restore any impairment his ego may have suffered:

1. *"Buck the line" intelligently*

If, after calmly reviewing and weighing all of the circumstances surrounding the situation he decides that success is reasonably possible in the same field of endeavor, he may first eliminate as fully as he can the things which caused his failure and then wholeheartedly try again and again, until he wins. This, where possible, is the best solution.

If, however, he decides that this is impossible or impractical, he has at least two other courses he may follow.

2. *Sublimation*

The first of these is what psychologists call sublimation, or the process of discovering for a desire not possible of attainment "a substitute outlet which proves in behavior to have a really equivalent value from the point of view of expressing and unifying personality."[1]

One may, for example, turn his energies to a different, *but similar* field of activity where there is more chance of winning and the satisfactions are somewhat similar. A girl who wants a stage career finds this impossible because of a birthmark, which mars her beauty, and so she takes up broadcasting. A boy who finds football impossible, takes up tennis, or golf. Each has found a way to eliminate any feeling of inferiority he or she may have felt by finding another equally healthful and desirable activity which offers much the same satisfactions.

If there is no readily available opportunity to do this, one may use his energy in an entirely different, but equally worthy field and win satisfaction by succeeding there; thus compensating for the disappointment, sometimes so fully that when he looks back years later he will realize that what seemed to be a misfortune was really a blessing. A boy who fails in athletics may serve his school and win popularity by being a successful member of the debating or dramatic team or by winning scholarship honors. Another boy may be handicapped by lameness, and may study to be a doctor and help thousands to avoid the disease which made him lame.

3. *Honest Defeat*

Occasionally it may even be wise for a person to admit frankly that he has lost, and that he just cannot have some one thing which he wanted, and to decide that he will be happy with what he can have and can do and that there will be no regrets, no bitterness.

These and similar "fact-facing" ways of meeting disappointments build sound, well-adjusted personalities. *These are not your problem cases.*

But the facts one must face after some humiliating experience or after having done something which, deep down in his heart,

[1] From *Human Nature and Management*, Ordway Tead (McGraw-Hill Book Co.).

he knows to be wrong, are not, as a rule, pleasant things. Often, too, the person's ego has been brought low by the experience and facing honestly such a fact as, for example, that the failure was due largely to his own carelessness and lack of preparation, is almost too much to bear. So he builds "defense mechanisms," as we call those methods of "defending" one's self, and restores his ego to something like its normal level without the painful necessity of having to correct his faults. These defense mechanisms fall into two broad types.

The first is an almost unconscious *regression to some form of behavior through which in the past, usually in childhood, the person has succeeded in getting what he wants.* Psychologists call this "regression to the infantile."

The most frequent manifestation of this type of defense of the ego is an exhibition of childish tantrums by flying into a rage (righteous indignation, the person will call it) when the ego seems to be in danger and, in this manner trying, consciously or unconsciously, to keep away any investigation by others, even by himself, which might reveal that the fault is right at home.

There is an old saying: "A woman will usually forgive you when *you* are wrong; but when *she* is wrong, never!"

Perhaps we might paraphrase that by saying that an employee with a grievance will almost always forgive his employer when investigation shows that the fault lies with the firm and the supervisor promises to straighten out matters; but the employee will often grow angry and refuse to listen to reason when it begins to look as if the supervisor is about to uncover the fact that the employee is the one at fault. And often this defense is so automatic that the employee fools himself with it more completely than he does the supervisor. Such cases call for careful and sympathetic handling. Perhaps the worst thing the supervisor can do is to try to *force* the employee to admit that the fault is his own.

Another childish defense mechanism is the habit of over emphasizing some one small accomplishment and always bringing it to the forefront whenever there seems to be any danger that someone else will get more glory than he is getting. The person who protects his ego by the use of this device will usually blame the organization or his supervisor for not valuing as highly as he should this skill. If, for example, there is an ability to do mental calculation rapidly, he will, whenever some one else is praised, call attention to the fact that he can add two columns of figures while the other person is adding only one.

Bragging and "showing off" in general are other forms of regression to the infantile and, like the boy who expands his ego by picking on smaller boys, the adult who delights in making other people feel small so that, by comparison, he can feel big, is always a coward at heart. He is one of the leader's most difficult problem cases.

Whining and complaining are other forms of childishness one sometimes sees in adults.

The other general type of defense mechanism takes the form of an attempt to *explain away the failure or disappointment* in some way which will satisfy the person himself that he is not at fault.

J. Pierpont Morgan has been credited with the statement that every man has two reasons for almost everything he does, a *good* one and the *real* one.

Practically every one indulges, at times, in the practice (called rationalization by psychologists) of seeking and finding plausible excuses for what he is doing or wishes to do, excuses which convince him that his conduct is thoroughly sound and rational and, if some one criticizes him, he may even build up and believe the fiction that what he is doing is really most commendable—that he is being grossly misunderstood. Usually these excuses convince only the person who makes them.

There are two ways in which the supervisor is interested in the practice of rationalization.

1. To be sure that he is not himself excusing *to himself* some of his own poor methods of supervision by some such statement as (almost a boast), "I believe in talking straight from the shoulder and not beating around the bush," when he is really just not willing to give the care and thought necessary to tactfulness.

2. To recognize this practice in others, and deal with it skillfully and understandingly. The excuses are often thoroughly sincere, and any attempt to treat them as insincere or as "alibis" will frequently accomplish nothing but to antagonize the person who makes them.

Possibly even more common than rationalization as an "explaining-away" method of protecting the ego is the habit of blaming someone else for every mistake, for everything unpleasant which happens. And it is so easy to do this. Probably nothing which happens to any person is entirely his own fault. Some of the blame does belong on the shoulders of someone else, and it is easy to decide that the one thing which was the fault of the other person was the principal cause of the trouble.

But whatever form the defense mechanism may take, the most important thing for the executive to remember as he attempts to get the person to come out from behind this artificial defense and to look the facts squarely in the face, is that, obvious as the fiction may appear to the executive, it is quite possible that the person is sincere in his belief that he is in the right. The executive must never forget that a person can usually fool himself more easily than he can fool anyone else.

Force can never correct a condition like this. Only sympathetic understanding and guidance can do it. Roughly jerking away the fiction which has been so carefully built up to protect the person's ego from impairment will, at best, only cause another fiction to be invented and believed. But if a different and socially acceptable method of assuring the protection of the ego is skillfully suggested, always without any attempt to force an admission that the other protection was a fiction, the bad form of behavior will often disappear naturally, as the need or supposed need for it disappears.

Responsibility of Parents, Teachers, and Supervisors

Parents, teachers, and supervisors can help to improve the personalities of those under their supervision by doing five things:

1. By *avoiding arbitrary rulings and peremptory orders*, especially in cases where the person may feel that the careful explanation of the reasons could and should be given.

2. By trying, whenever it is necessary to introduce a disappointment, also *to suggest tactfully and skillfully a sound compensating activity* which will prove to have an equivalent value in satisfying the real wants of the person.

3. By trying, when correcting poor behavior of any type, *to find just what want that behavior is an attempt to satisfy;* and

then offering a more desirable substitute activity which will satisfy the same want.

4. By endeavoring *to keep as fully in the background as is possible their own natural desire to enhance their own egos* by some unnecessary show of authority, by display of personal knowledge or skill, by accepting unearned applause, or in any other way.

5. By studying their own personalities as objectively as is possible so as *to discover and eliminate anything in their behavior toward those under their supervision which has in it any "hang-overs" from their own disappointments*, or any tendency to rationalize and excuse their own poor methods of supervision.

Steps in Handling a Complaint or Grievance

Always try first to reach the real cause of the complaint or grievance. More often than not, it is based on a misunderstanding or a disappointment and if that misunderstanding can be removed or a satisfactory substitute which will alleviate the disappointment can be found, the trouble is eliminated. Go as deeply into the person's background of training and experience and family history as you can without too much questioning. Is there any bitterness from past social injustices (real or fancied)? What is the fundamental cause of any warped attitude?

Get all of the facts before expressing your own opinion. Listen attentively and patiently to the person's whole story. Often this story, supplemented by the answers to a few questions skillfully put, will give you enough information so that you can "see both sides." Sometimes all that will be necessary will be to give tactfully some general advice and an explanation as to how the misunderstanding "might have happened," and then to say, "Will you give me a day or two on this? I think, if you will, I can work out a solution for you. In the meantime will you try your best to do even a little more than your part . . . ?"

After a few days the person should be sent for again. It is surprising to note how often in that two or three days the whole thing will have worked itself out. Just your listening patiently and your advice as to what "might have caused the trouble" have removed the trouble. If so, let the matter drop. If not, you now have more facts on which to proceed.

No matter how unreasonable the complaint, try to maintain to the end a friendly, helpful, impersonal attitude.

Finally, if after all reasonable effort has been made to correct the employee's attitude he continues to make unreasonable complaints and to have difficulties with people in the department, the only practical solution of the problem is a dismissal. No department can afford to retain a chronic trouble maker.

Special Methods for Specific Problems

Conceit (*bluff*). Conceit is of two kinds. The more common is that which is really an effort to hide ignorance or fear. A better term for this type would be "bluff," which is defined as "bold speech or manner intended to overawe or deceive."

In correcting this type of apparent conceit, the supervisor should recognize the fact that the primary cause is, usually, poor leadership in the past experience of the person. He has, probably, frankly admitted his ignorance, and has been "bawled out" for it. The next time he has "bluffed it through," counting on getting the information in time to avoid detection, and has "got away with it." There is so much of this poor type of supervision that it is not surprising that the type of so-called conceit which it causes is perhaps the most common failing the leader will encounter.

The natural approach to a correction of this fault is to show the person that bluffing is not necessary, and this can and should be done without trying to "show up" the person's bluff or ignorance.

A method which has been used successfully when some person says in a rather boastful way that he is "all set" for some situation, or "has it in the bag," is for the supervisor to say frankly, "Well, this is a subject we probably all have much to learn about. Let's go over your plans together; maybe you can help me some and I can help you some." The supervisor sets the example by admitting that he has something to learn. Then, as he goes over the plans, he will probably find place after place where the person is not "all set"; but there should be no "bawling out" or "just as I thought." If the person is of the right sort, this will not be necessary. Of course, if after a lesson or two of this type the person continues to bluff, then a plain, straight-from-the-shoulder talk on the subject will be necessary.

Conceit (*overconfidence in own ability or knowledge, usually accompanied by boastful expressions or actions*). The person who shows this type of conceit usually has some ability. Often, too, success has come rapidly, due partly to ability and partly to fortunate chance.

The best method of approach in such cases is, probably, a frank talk, admitting the person's ability, but pointing out the fact that talking about this will antagonize people and sooner or later cause failure. If necessary, just which part of his success has been due to chance may be called to his attention. Also, the person should be encouraged to set higher standards for himself, and measure his achievement against that of those who have done outstandingly well, rather than against the accomplishments of those who have really not achieved anything worth while.

Some executives assert that the most successful method is to "show up" the person; to give him an assignment which he cannot successfully complete, and let him fail. If it is then possible to give the same assignment to someone who has had less education or experience, but who can do that job well, this will add to the effectiveness of the cure. This method is so likely to antagonize an employee and do permanent damage to his personality that it is unwise except as a last resort.

Cure conceit not by killing self-confidence, but by raising standards.

Sensitiveness. The person whose feelings are too easily hurt presents a difficult problem, and yet he is often one of the most valuable employees in the department. Probably the first step in the correction of oversensitiveness is to endeavor to understand what causes sensitiveness. People who are sensitive are usually so because they have more exacting standards of some kind than those who are not so, and they are offended by the failure of others to adhere to these standards. Usually they are people of rather keen intellects and find sensibilities. The truly sensitive person who can retain his keenness of feeling and his fine sense of fairness and justice, but learn also to understand that all blunt or careless remarks are not meant as insults, is the ideal type for development in most public contact positions.

A quiet, friendly, tactful talk on the subject will usually be helpful in correcting oversensitiveness. As a rule, too, the opportunity for this talk will be made by the person who is sensitive, and it will not be necessary for the supervisor to start the discussion himself.

Care should be taken to begin the discussion with a statement of the person's good points. "But there is one thing which, I think, is really holding you back. Would you like to know what that one thing is?"

Stubbornness. The stubborn person has some strength of character, or he would not be stubborn. He is worth saving.

Almost always there is a reason and, to the person at least, a very good reason, for his thinking he should not do a certain thing. He may think the rule petty and that it has no bearing on his job efficiency.

"We certainly do not mean to ask you to do anything which it is not reasonable to ask, and (smilingly) if your reason for not doing this is better than ours for thinking you should do it, we are not going to ask you to do it. You tell me your reason and I will tell you ours, and I think we can reach an agreement." And usually you can.

Of course, this method presupposes that there is a carefully thought-out and fully logical reason for every rule and requirement. And there should be. If there is not, thank the stubborn person for pointing out the unreasonableness of the rule, and try to get the rule changed.

The worried employee. It would be difficult to estimate how much loss in efficiency and how many accidents are caused by worry, but the loss to production from this cause is considerable. The worried employee is neither an efficient employee nor a safe employee.

Of course, worry can never be completely eliminated, but skillful and sympathetic supervision can greatly reduce it and, even in cases where it would seem that nothing the supervisor can do will help, it is surprising how much just the knowledge that the supervisor knows and understands and sympathizes will help.

The first step in helping the worried employee should be taken before the employee begins to worry. That step is the establishment of a friendly relationship between supervisor and employee in which the supervisor grows to know something about the employee's life outside the shop—how his children are doing in school, what are his hobbies, whether or not he is buying a home. All of this can be done naturally and easily without prying; and lays the foundation for the best help when he becomes worried (see Chapter IV).

The next step is to recognize the symptoms of worry so as to know when help is needed. In many cases, if the proper foundation of friendly relationship is established, the employee will come to the supervisor at once and ask for his advice and help. But there will be those who do not feel that they want to worry the supervisor with their personal problems and will not ask. Usually, however, there will be some marked change in behavior which the alert supervisor will notice. A man who usually whistles at his work, suddenly stops; a girl may be even more gay than usual, but there seems to be something forced about it; a man who has never used alcoholic beverages to excess, shows evidence of doing so; a man who is usually alert seems preoccupied and must be spoken to more than once before he hears; a girl who has always been pleasant to work with becomes irritable and snaps at her associates and the supervisor; a man suddenly is absent or late more than usual.

All of these are symptoms which, to the alert supervisor, mean that something is wrong, and his next step is to find out what that something is. A friendly question and offer of assistance if needed will usually bring the desired response.

The things employees worry about most frequently are:

1. Whether or not they are making good on the job.
2. Rumors that there will be a lot of layoffs or that for some other reason the job will not be permanent.
3. Unpleasant relations with fellow employees.
4. Bad physical working conditions.
5. Problems at home, such as health of wife or children, financial problems, domestic relations problems.

The first four difficulties can as a rule be handled directly by the supervisor. To take care of the fifth properly the supervisor will often have to ask for assistance. If he does not know just where to get this assistance his personnel director, or the employee counselor can tell him, and also can help him with the problem.

The older employee. The number of older employees in every business seems to be increasing and it is not just a temporary condition. The percentage of our population over fifty years of age has been increasing during the past twenty or thirty years and will probably continue to increase. There are, and probably will continue to be, more "older employees" in every business organization. The limited number of jobs to which we have regularly transferred people of advanced years is becoming increasingly inadequate.

Also, many older people were thrown out of work during the depression or have lost their jobs because of business failures. The old man in your department working as a junior clerk may have been the head bookkeeper of a large firm which was forced to close its doors. The man who sweeps the shop floor may have been a trusted stockkeeper in some large manufacturing plant.

Finally, the percentage of college graduates competing for even the less important jobs in business and industry has increased greatly in the past ten or fifteen years. The man past fifty in your department did not have the opportunity that you had to take a college course which would fit him for business. In his younger days he probably received little encouragement to study. Most business executives at that time were recommending their own alma mater, the "school of hard knocks."

It is not surprising, then, that often we find in the older employee a feeling of bitterness and despair. He feels that the fault lies with someone other than himself. Often, too, a resentful or a bored attitude toward instruction is assumed purely as a "defense mechanism," to hide fear of dismissal or the natural dislike of admitting ignorance of anything to a younger person and asking advice and help of that younger person. This is especially true if the supervisor is much younger and has only recently been promoted to an executive position.

One of the simplest and best ways to eliminate any feeling of resentment is for the supervisor to ask the older employee for help—to make him more of a partner than a subordinate. A salesman seventy-five years old persisted in violating minor new rules which it had become necessary to make because the business had increased in size. The supervisor was thirty-two years old. Here was his approach:

"Mr. Thompson, I want to get you to help me with a problem I have. You know that there is a rule that every sale must be. . . . Frankly, this rule was not made for you, because we all know you have judgment enough to know when to follow it and when not to follow it; but that is not true of the younger salespeople in the department and, quite naturally, they look to you as a leader. When they see you doing something they think it must be all right. Now what I want you to do for me, if you will, is to follow this rule exactly, not so much because the management has any fear of your making a mistake, but because we both know that serious consequences are likely to follow if we let the bars down generally."

This same approach was used successfully by a young safety engineer to get older mechanics to observe certain safety rules, such as always wearing goggles when grinding tools.

The whole technique of handling the older employee may be summed up in three simple rules:

1. Make him feel that he is a partner rather than an employee. Ask his advice and help about things he knows, and do not hesitate to do this in public. Let there be the feeling: "You know many things from your long experience which will help me; I know some of the newer methods and some of the specialized information about this department which will help you. Let's be partners, and exchange information and helpfulness."

2. Be especially careful, even more so than is necessary with the younger employee, to make any correction, or even to give any instructions, as privately as possible.

3. Make friendly inquiry from time to time about some son or daughter or other relative who has been successful. I remember an old man who had been forced by circumstances to take a minor position. The supervisor found it difficult to penetrate beyond the wall he had built around himself, until the former chanced to find out that the old man had a son in West Point who was graduating that year within two or three places of being at the head of the class.

A Statement of Personnel Policy

Many firms have found it to be of great assistance in their efforts to keep to a minimum any causes for grievances, to prepare most carefully, and with the aid of the employees themselves, a statement of Personnel Policy.

When the policy is clearly presented in writing, both supervisor and employee know exactly what are their rights and powers and there is usually no desire on the part of either to go beyond his rights; but when neither understands just what are the rights and powers of the other, it is only natural that there should be misunderstandings. And misunderstandings usually lead to grievances, expressed, or, what is often worse, unexpressed.

Most of the firms which have prepared statements of personnel policy have incorporated these statements in their booklets of information for employees so as to secure as wide distribution as possible. The statement which follows is a composite of the statements of several organizations:

The Personnel Policy of the Blank Company

The keynote of the whole policy of management is a constant endeavor to achieve *fairness*. All rules and procedures have as a major purpose an effort to make sure that all persons in any way connected with the operation of the business—customers, employees, management, and stockholders—will be treated fairly and with due consideration for their feelings.

Our personnel policy, in harmony with this general policy, is briefly stated in the following paragraphs:

1. Selection for employment and for promotion is made on the basis of merit and fitness for the job. The aim in every case is to place each person in the kind of work best suited to his abilities.
2. When filling any position in the organization, first consideration is given to present employees who are qualified, and for whom transfer to the position is advantageous. Vacancies are filled by the employment of persons from the outside only when their qualifications are more specifically suited to the requirements of the positions or are superior

to the qualifications of employees available within the organization.

3. Every effort is made to see that employees who do work of similar difficulty and responsibility are classified in equivalent salary grades. Pay increases within the limits of established ranges are based on efficiency and merit, ascertained by systematic reviews.
4. Salary ranges for all positions are set, taking into account the difficulty of the work, amount of special training or number of skills required, and whether or not the work requires aptitudes or abilities which are unusual. The complete schedule of salary ranges is published in this handbook and any employee is at liberty to discuss at any time with his supervisor or with the personnel director any questions he may have as to the justice of the salary range of his position or of any other position.
5. Supervisors are responsible for giving employees all reasonable assistance in their efforts to become proficient in their work and to prepare for advancement. Training given by supervisors is supplemented when necessary by added facilities. Half of the tuition paid is refunded to employees who complete satisfactorily certain evening courses.
6. Once each six months all supervisors are asked to review carefully the work of the people under their supervision and to rate them on quality of work, volume of work, capacity to develop, initiative, work attitude, attitude towards others, and knowledge of the work. These reports are carefully reviewed by a committee made up of the department head, personnel director, and supervisor. A report is given to each employee telling exactly how he has been rated, and he is invited to discuss this with his supervisor or the personnel director.
7. Continued effort is made to maintain healthful, sanitary, and safe working conditions.
8. It is to the interest of management and employee alike that all employees be granted regular annual vacations with pay and leave with pay during reasonable periods of inability to work because of illness or injury. It is the duty of the

employee to use these periods of absence in a manner which will build up his health and efficiency.

9. It is the aim of the management to co-operate in and aid in financing, but in no way to dominate, all athletic or other recreational activities in which any considerable group of employees is interested.
10. The question of joining any legal organization or association of employees is one for individual employees to decide for themselves. Employees will not be discriminated against nor receive preferential treatment because of membership or lack of membership in any such organization or association.
11. Employees are encouraged to discuss freely with executives any matters concerning their welfare and to suggest improvements in methods, procedures, and working conditions. Careful consideration is given all suggestions and suitable cash rewards are offered for suggestions which are accepted.
12. It is the responsibility of supervisors, officials, and employees to avoid as fully as possible conditions which give rise to grievances of any kind. When, however, there is a feeling on the part of any employee that any condition is unfair, he should always feel free to present his case either to his own supervisor, to the officer in charge of his department, or to the personnel director. All such requests for hearings will be given prompt consideration and every facility given the employee for appealing to higher authority any decision which he believes to be unfair. The procedure for such appeal is described in detail later in this handbook.
13. Continued employment requires that employees shall render honest, efficient, and loyal service. If an employee who is doing his honest best is unsuited for the tasks to which he is assigned, efforts are made to place him at other work for which he is suited. Selection for layoff or reassignment because of reduction, conclusion, or rearrangement of work, is made on the basis of merit.
14. When it is necessary for reasons other than the employee's own misconduct to terminate the services of any employee,

other than a temporary employee, not less than one week of notice will be given for each year of continuous service, with a maximum of eight weeks, or pay for an equal period in lieu of notice.

15. No person in a supervisory position is permitted at any time to accept any gift or present from any employee or group of employees under his supervision; nor may he borrow money from any such employee or obtain the signature of such employee as endorser or co-maker of any note offered as security for a loan.

It is the responsibility of every officer, supervisor, and employee to make these policies fully effective in the course of actual operations and to carry on the daily work of the organization in a spirit of friendliness.

A more detailed statement of the privileges and responsibilities of all employees is usually given in the part of the handbook that follows this statement of general personnel policy.

Suggested Supplementary Reading on the Supervisor's Problem Cases

It has been impossible, because of the limitations of space, to discuss in detail the various types and causes of abnormal behavior and distorted thinking. A careful study of the chapters suggested in the six books listed below is strongly recommended. This study will help the supervisor to understand better the underlying reasons for certain faults he is trying to correct in those under his supervision, and will often point to a satisfactory method of correction. The books should, if possible, be read in the order named.

Human Nature and Management, Ordway Tead.

Chapter IX, What are the Defense Mechanisms, gives an explanation of the causes of many cases of distorted thinking.

About Ourselves, H. A. Overstreet.

A discussion of abnormal behavior written on the assumption that no one is absolutely "normal" and that "it may help us to see our smaller ills projected on to the silver sheet of abnormal behavior." The book is written in popular style with little use of technical terminology.

Psychiatry in Industry, V. V. Anderson.

Dr. Anderson was for a number of years director of Medical Research at Macy's. This book is largely based on studies made in that store. Chapter II is a study of work failures and their treatment.

Human Nature at Work, Jean L. Shepard.

Chapter VI, On the Job: Criticism (pp. 118–128), tells the story of two cases and makes some general suggestions.

The Technique of Executive Control, E. H. Schell.

Chapters X–XIII discuss the following executive difficulties:

With subordinates: Open opposition, covert opposition, sullenness, stubbornness, discourtesy, disloyalty, prejudice, conceit, dishonesty, immorality, uncertainty, worry, fear, grief, irresponsibility, unreliability, dullness, lack of perseverance, lack of initiative, religious difficulties, differences due to nationality, social differences, family differences, and difficulties due to wages.

With associates: The newcomer, plant politics, cliques, technical difficulties, responsibility for errors, changes in rank, overambitiousness, pompousness, plain meanness, difficulties caused by worry and fatigue, age differences, social responsibilities, and religious and race differences.

With superiors: Disagreement with orders, appeal to higher officials, delays in decisions, incompatibility, assumed mistreatment, and external relationships.

The New Techniques for Supervisors and Foremen, Albert Walton.

Chapter 7, Personality, and Chapter 11, Normal and Abnormal.

"Helping the Worried Worker," in *Personnel*, September, 1944.

This article is adapted from a fuller treatment of the subject in *Industrial Mental Health*, a manual issued by the Michigan Industrial Mental Health Council and the State Board of Control for Vocational Education.

CHAPTER XV

How to Handle Dismissals

About forty years ago I was a timekeeper. It became necessary to lay off fifteen or twenty men out of a force of about one hundred. On payday the superintendent stood at my shoulder, and as the men to be laid off came to the window for their pay envelopes he merely said to each, "We won't need you any more." In the envelope was the dreaded "pink slip" which so often, in those days, was the only notice of dismissal.

Crude as this old method was, it is no worse than that followed by many executives today. One head of a large manufacturing business wished to dismiss an engineer whose services had not been satisfactory. He so dreaded the interview that he went to New York on a business trip that he persuaded himself was necessary and left a brief note for his secretary to give to the engineer. Many department heads who really have a genuine feeling of sympathy for the person who must go so steel themselves for the dreaded interview that when the time comes they seem blunt and heartless.

No task in supervision is more unpleasant than that of telling an employee his services are no longer needed. As a result, no part of supervision is more often poorly handled.

Everyone who accepts the responsibility for directing the work of others should know that, sooner or later, it will be his task to tell someone that he must look for another job. The supervisor should not shirk this task. He should, rather, try to learn how to perform his unpleasant duty in a manner that will let the person leave with his self-respect unimpaired, and with a feeling that he has been fairly and justly treated.

This can be done in nine cases out of ten if the supervisor will be careful to follow a few simple suggestions.

First of all, he should be sure he is right in his recommendation of dismissal. If the cause is a reduction of force he should have factual knowledge back of the selection of who is to be laid off. If the reason is that the person cannot do the work, the executive should check carefully to see if the employee has had proper training, proper equipment, and reasonable time in which to learn.

Above all, the action must be fair, or no amount of "technique" can send the person away without resentment.

Next, the person must be told. The interview should not be hurried. It should be private. After the person has come in and is seated, the executive should waste no time in announcing the reason for the interview. Considerable thought should, however, be given to just what words to use, always remembering the objective—no impairment of courage, self-respect, or good will toward the firm.

A statement about like this has been used many times, with good results:

"Mr. Smith, you and I have talked together several times about your work. I am sure you have done the best you can, but I don't believe this is the right type of work for you, and I believe the wisest thing for you to do is to look for another job. I have been authorized to give you four weeks' notice so you will have a chance to find something. You will be on the payroll for the four weeks, but you may have just as much time off as you may need. If I were you I would start out tomorrow and look for something. If I can help in any way, I shall be very glad to do so. Don't hesitate to ask me to do anything I can."

Often the man will ask for advice as to which line of work you would suggest. This should be given carefully, with, if possible, some suggestions as to where work of this kind might be obtained. Possibly an appointment may be arranged over the telephone and, although one appointment does not make a job, it does do much to bolster up courage.

One large manufacturing company found it necessary to lay off over a thousand men and women during 1931. Virtually the entire personnel department was turned into a "placement bureau." Each employee was interviewed carefully to find what other types of work he might do. The community for ten miles around was canvassed for jobs. As a result, a large percentage of all who were laid off found jobs. All of this probably cost twenty or twenty-five thousand dollars, but it was worth it many times over. A few years later that plant and all the other plants in the community were in need of good employees. The cream of the supply went to the plant which had been fair and considerate when the employees most needed fairness and consideration.

Treat resentment patiently. Sometimes the person being dismissed will be bitter, even to the point of criticizing you severely. If there is any one time when you can afford to be gracious and overlook almost anything, it is at this time. You should try calmly to show the person where he is mistaken and, if you do not succeed and the person starts to leave, invite him to come back to see you again in a few days. You do not want anyone to leave the organization feeling bitter.

The Separation Register

In order to eliminate as completely as possible all factors other than merit in any layoffs necessary in times of slack business, some organizations prepare "separation registers" in which are listed names of all employees who might be affected by the layoff. A separate register is prepared for each trade or occupation in which layoffs are necessary. It is decided in advance what factors are to be taken into account in deciding who is to be laid off and what shall be the "weight" of each factor.

Each employee is then rated on each factor and those having the lowest total scores on each register are the ones chosen for layoff. Names of veterans whose jobs are protected by law or regulation of the firm are not listed on these registers.

A typical list of factors and the weights assigned to each follows:

Service or Merit Rating. A number of points equal to the numerical score, average of the last two ratings.

Length of Service. Two points for each year, first five years; one point for each succeeding year.

Dependents. Five points for the first, two points for each succeeding dependent, as listed on income tax exemption certificate.

Absentee record. Deduction of two points for each one per cent of absence (other than vacation or temporary layoff) in excess of average (shop and office figured separately).

Military Service in Wartime. Ten points if the person was an employee of the firm just before entering the service; five points if not (requirements of the law will, of course, be met).

If your firm follows such a practice in deciding upon who shall be laid off, your task in convincing the employee that he has been treated fairly will be greatly simplified.

Suggested Supplementary Reading on How to Handle Dismissals

Personnel Administration, Tead and Metcalf.
Chapter XVI, Shop Rules, Grievances, and Discharge (pp. 230–233).

Human Nature at Work, Jean L. Shepard.
Chapter VI, On the Job: Criticism (pp. 128–134).

CHAPTER XVI

Developing an Assistant

THE training of an assistant or understudy is a task to which each supervisor should give careful thought and conscientious effort. It is one of his important duties. A few suggestions follow:

Select carefully. If you are to select a new assistant, be careful to select someone with such qualities that, with proper training and experience, he will be able to do the work you are now doing. If you feel that your present assistant does not have the possibility of development, talk over the matter with the executive under whom you work. He may be able either to help you develop your present assistant by means of special training, or to arrange a transfer for him so that you can select another assistant.

Teach the job thoroughly. The first step toward giving your assistant responsibility is to let him know as much as possible about everything you are doing. Talk over all of your plans with him; let him know your reasons for each decision.

Ask his opinion. As frequently as possible get your assistant's opinion on any matter under discussion, before you give your opinion. Ask his reasons for each opinion given. This will give him exercise in thinking for himself, and will enable you to know whether or not he has good judgment.

Build a feeling of responsibility. Build up a feeling of responsibility by letting him be entirely responsible for a certain part of the work. Let him plan how this work is to be assigned, make the assignments, and see that the work is carried out.

In the things which you have assigned to your assistant keep out as much as possible. Of course, you must retain general supervision, but the more fully you let your assistant do the job himself, even if he makes a few mistakes, the more quickly you will have an assistant who can take responsibility if necessary.

If you see an employee doing anything the wrong way and find that he is following the instructions of your assistant, do not reverse such instructions yourself, but explain quietly to your assistant which is the right way, and let him change his own instructions.

"Back up" your assistant. If he issues certain instructions and they are not followed, consider it as serious as if the instructions had been your own.

Never criticize publicly. Never criticize your assistant in the hearing of others. Little slighting remarks, such as "I wish I had done that myself" or "It does look as if he could have got that right," destroy the respect that the employees have for your assistant and make his success virtually impossible. You may have a poor assistant, but you will only make him worse by such treatment.

Be frank. Be perfectly frank, however, in your criticism and suggestions when you are alone with your assistant. If he really desires to "make good" he will not only take no offense at criticism, but will appreciate it because no one can improve unless told exactly where he is falling short. About the most unfair thing you can do to your assistant is to let him go serenely along without any suggestion that he may not be doing everything he should, and then to go to the management with the statement that he is unsatisfactory and that you request his transfer or dismissal.

Give praise when deserved. Give an occasional word of praise where praise is deserved, but be careful not to be too lavish in your bestowal of praise. If you praise him for every little thing that is done well, your praise will mean nothing. But when praise is really earned, give it. If your assistant makes a suggestion and you adopt it, give him credit for it when you put it into effect. Also, in your report to the management, give him credit, and let him know that you have done so.

Suggested Supplementary Reading on Developing an Assistant

The Art of Leadership, Ordway Tead.

Chapter XI, Problems of the Assistant Leader.

CHAPTER XVII

Special Considerations in the Supervision of Women

SOMEONE has said that exactly the same rules apply in the supervision of women as in the supervision of men—*only more so!*

There is probably no better way to state the exact situation than that. We should be careful always to be courteous and considerate of the employee's feelings; to notice and say a word of praise about any work done especially well or unusual effort expended; to avoid meticulously any evidence of liking one employee better than another; to explain in advance any changes which will affect the employee; and to do all of the other things, especially the little things, which make the employee happy on the job. And we should do these things whether we are supervising men or women. But if we do grow a little careless about some of them, the adverse effect on the work and attitude will probably be less serious if our employees are men than if they are women.

So perhaps no new rules are necessary in this chapter, just an explanation of why careful following of certain rules and suggestions already given is even more important when supervising women than when supervising men.

Probably the most important difference between men and women, from the supervisor's viewpoint, is the fact that the man expects to work at some gainful occupation all of his life, while for women the job is, more frequently than not, merely a temporary matter until she meets the right man and gets married. At most she expects to work only until she and her husband together can save enough to buy the furniture and other things they need. Of course, many women do work all of their lives and many are more interested in careers than in marriage; but for the majority this is not true.

Some conclusions as to the things women consider important in a job as related to the things men consider important were brought out in the "Hawthorne Experiment."[1] The conclusions reached were based on 6,800 interviews with men and 3,500 with women.

An analysis of what men and women talked about shows that the men were interested primarily in those things related to economic security (life insurance, pensions, employment) and advancement (education and advancement).

Women, on the other hand, were more interested in thrift, welfare, overtime, rest periods, fatigue, social contacts, furniture. The conclusion reached was that what the average woman wants is "an easy job, not too fatiguing, in pleasant surroundings, sufficiently well paid to support herself or to contribute to the income of her parents or husband, and congenial hours which allow her to take part in the activities of the home."

Women are much more concerned than are men about the general neatness and cleanliness of surroundings, *especially of washrooms.*

Many plants have found that follow-up by a personnel department should be sooner in the case of women, because the new woman is usually making a greater change than the new man. Often she is on an entirely new type of work calling for the exercise of muscles she has not used. She is likely to get discouraged unless it is explained to her that the excessive fatigue will soon pass. The medical departments in some plants suggest specific exercises for each type of work.

Women are more likely than are men to become unhappy in the early days of employment if they do not almost immediately make what they consider to be proper progress in learning the job. They need encouragement and assurance that they are doing all right much more frequently than do men.

Women, too, are more affected by whether or not the group seems to like them. If it does not appear that a woman is going to be accepted by the group, a transfer to another department, preceded if possible by some suggestions from a woman counse-

[1] See *Management and the Worker*, Roethlisberger and Dickson, p. 245, (Harvard University Press).

lor, will often save the day. A woman is not nearly so willing as a man to remain in a department where she does not seem to be at least reasonably popular.

All of this means that the supervisor will have to give more time and sympathetic understanding to the induction of women employees than is usually considered necessary in the case of men.

The experience with brief rest periods, usually ten minutes morning and afternoon, is almost universally favorable. There is usually some actual increase in output in spite of the reduction in time worked. Also, there is usually a marked improvement in the quality of work.

A study of the relative merits of praising, reproving, and ignoring the person being supervised is described in Chapter IV.

It will be remembered that the results were 71 per cent improvement for the group which was praised, 20 per cent for the group which was reproved and 5 per cent for the group that was ignored. But let us see how the three methods affected boys and girls separately.

	Girls			*Boys*		
	First Test	*Fifth Test*	*Per Cent Improvement*	*First Test*	*Fifth Test*	*Per Cent Improvement*
Praised Group	10.73	19.93	86	13.16	20.58	54
Reproved Group	10.73	12.20	14	13.25	16.66	26
Ignored Group	10.60	11.33	7	13.54	13.82	2

While, of course, the results of this test are by no means conclusive, they do seem to point to the fact that skillful use of the "praise technique" (discussed in Chapter IV) is outstandingly the best method to use in the supervision of women. And this is borne out by experience of almost every successful supervisor of women I have talked with on this subject.

And so we come back to the opening statement of this chapter: *Exactly the same rules apply in the supervision of women as in the supervision of men*—ONLY MORE SO!

Hiring Women for Production Jobs

The Woman's Bureau of the United States Department of Labor, in special Bulletin Number 14, makes these suggestions to employers hiring women for production jobs:

1. Sell the idea of women workers to present employee staff —the foremen and men workers.
2. Survey jobs to decide which are most suitable for women.
3. Make adaptations of jobs to fit smaller frames and lesser muscular strength of women.
4. Provide service facilities in the plant to accommodate anticipated number of women.
5. Appoint a woman personnel director to organize and head a woman-counselor system.
6. Select women carefully and for specific jobs.
7. Develop a program for the induction and training of women.
8. Establish good working conditions.
9. Supervise women workers intelligently.
10. Give women equal opportunity with men.

The Woman Supervisor[2]

There are many women supervisors in all types of business and this number seems destined to grow larger; and there is no reason why these women cannot be as successful as men in the field of supervision. In fact, as the old strong-arm methods of supervision disappear and the supervisor who would be successful must be more of an influencer and a teacher than a boss and commander, many feminine traits become assets rather than liabilities.

But to be successful, the woman supervisor must overcome the prejudice against "working under a woman" voiced by many women as well as men.

Perhaps the best way for each woman supervisor to overcome this in her own case is to review carefully the charges against women supervisors in general which women workers have made in defense of their own aversion to working for women. And as each criticism is read, the supervisor will do well to consider carefully whether or not the charge is true in her case. If it is she should take steps to correct it.[3]

[2] The discussion under this heading is based largely on Chapter XIII, Problems of Women Leaders, in *The Art of Leadership*, by Ordway Tead. (McGraw-Hill Book Co.).

[3] The man supervisor, also, will profit from reading this list of poor supervision practices. He may find that he is guilty of some of them even though they are supposed to be essentially feminine in character.

One of the most frequent complaints is that women supervisors "do not give sufficient credit to those who work with them." There seems to be a feeling on the part of the supervisor that to give too much credit for results to those under her will make her own position less secure. And with everyone "gunning" for the woman supervisor it is not surprising that she should be inclined to defend her position too zealously, even jealously. But it is a tendency the woman supervisor must recognize as bad, and guard against.

This same tendency is probably the cause of the criticism, occasionally heard that women supervisors do not like to have those under them "get too good" or "try to get ahead too fast."

Frequently heard, also, is the complaint that women supervisors are "too personal." They do not seem to be able to make the necessary distinction between loyalty to the aims of the organization and loyalty to themselves. They like constant expressions of loyalty to themselves, and may become offended if these are omitted.

Women supervisors, again, are said to be "too fussy and particular and prying." They over-supervise. They do not seem to be able to assign a job with proper instructions and then leave the person alone. This is even true, or at least so say many women workers, in their supervision of experienced people who know how to do the job. This tendency to interfere during the execution of a task is most annoying because it is a direct attack on the ego of the worker. And yet some check upon the progress of the work must be made. Knowing just how much checking is necessary for each worker, and doing just that much and no more, is one of the difficult parts of supervision.

Women supervisors are often too skeptical of their women workers, frequently making some such remark as this: "The girls can put it over on the men supervisors with their charms, but not on me—I know them too well." The making of such remarks, even though in some cases they are true, antagonizes the sincere, loyal, and hard-working woman in the section and certainly does nothing to correct the attitude of those who for years, sometimes unconsciously, have largely got by on their "charm" rather than by hard and conscientious work.

A final criticism is: "Working for a woman is not exciting

enough. We like to have some men around." When one realizes how frequently a woman's work setting may be the best normal means for her to meet and associate with men who have jobs and are making good livings, it will be seen that this is by no means a trivial matter. The woman supervisor in charge of a section made up largely or entirely of women workers may find it a difficult problem to make working in the section a satisfying social experience as well as a means of making a livelihood; but this is a problem for which she must find a solution if she is to be fully successful as a supervisor.

Suggested Supplementary Reading on the Supervision of Women

Bulletins of The Woman's Bureau, U.S. Department of Labor.
Some bulletins are: When You Hire Women; Recreation and Housing for Women War Workers; The Industrial Nurse and the Woman Worker; The Effect of Rest Periods on Output; and Employing Women in Shipyards.

The Art of Leadership, Ordway Tead.
Chapter XIII, The Problems of Women Leaders.

CHAPTER XVIII

Two-Way Communication

KNOWING and understanding the other person's point of view—his needs, his problems, his emotional hungers—is the only dependable foundation for intelligent and happy human relations.

This fact has long been recognized by management; but all too often in the past and in too many cases even now, those on the management side of the picture have taken a one-sided view of the problem. Our thinking has too often been, "If the worker could only understand and appreciate management's problems and needs."

It is important, most important, that the worker should understand management's problems and needs. But it is equally important that management should understand the worker's problems and needs—the pressures brought on him by increasing costs; the fears that he may lose his job through arbitrary and uncontrolled action by some one person; the deep-seated hunger for recognition and for a feeling that he is a *member*, not merely a *servant*, of the enterprise; the resentments built up by real or imagined unfair treatment in the past.

So we find an ever increasing number of business organizations doing two things: (1) trying to find out what the worker believes about management and what are the wants he expects his job to satisfy for him and (2) trying to tell management's story to the worker in a way that takes into account the worker's wants (just as the Washington *Star* advertisement quoted in Chapter III mentioned the reader's wants first).

WHAT THE WORKER WANTS

The general manager of any organization needs to know more than what workers in general believe and want. If he is to do an intelligent job of managing the enterprise, he must know specifically what the workers in his own organization believe about the way things are being run. He needs especially to know what things are not being done for them which they believe should be done. The means most frequently used to get such information is of an attitude survey, in which employees are asked to fill out questionnaires.

Attitude Surveys

The usual procedure is to gather employees together in groups and seat them so each employee can fill out the questionnaire without other employees being able to see his answers. Questionnaires are unsigned, and questions are answered by checking the desired statement after each question; this avoids any identification of the employee. Tabulation of replies is made by an outside organization. Often the entire survey is conducted and interpreted by a consulting firm specializing in this type of work.

Another method of getting the information, which many believe to better than having employees fill out questionnaires, is to have trained interviewers call at homes throughout the community and ask questions designed to find out the community's attitude toward the employment practices of the particular company and of other similar organizations. The interviewers do not know what organization is sponsoring the survey.

One important advantage of this type of survey is that it shows the organization's standing in relation to other organizations in the community; and it is this relative standing which it is most important for the management to know.

Will management listen?

This may seem a foolish question, but it is not. Too often management is so certain that its opinions about what employees believe and want are right that it refuses to listen when the message coming in "doesn't sound reasonable." I have actually known companies to spend considerable sums of money on attitude surveys and then dismiss the findings, which were unpleasant but which were later proved to be correct, with some such comment as, "I know better than that; the interviewer must have talked to some 'sore head.' "

Management—and that means all of us from the supervisor of a small group to the general manager—must be willing to listen as well as talk if two-way communication is to be successful. This is not so easy as it sounds. Criticism is harder to take than praise, but is often much more profitable.

How Management Tells its Story

Letters and bulletins to employees

Management must think and speak in terms of *what the employees want* if it expects its messages to accomplish anything more worth while than to serve as kindling in the employee's furnace or fireplace.

If it is at all practicable, these wants should be determined by some form of attitude survey. If this is not practicable, the next best thing is to think in terms of the wants of employees in general as determined by other such surveys. Among these wants are: (1) to have a feeling of security; (2) to be treated fairly; (3) to have an opportunity to gain individual recognition and distinction; (4) to have a relationship with foremen and fellow workers which is pleasant, harmonious, and friendly; and finally (5) to know something about what is going on, whether the news is encouraging or discouraging.

Many programs start with a letter from the president of the company discussing conditions and asking for suggestions. These letters are usually mailed to the employees' homes. The last sentence in such a letter by the president of the International Harvester Company set the basic policy for the program of that company, a policy which any company might well adopt. The policy is: "With minor and temporary exceptions, we have no secrets and will talk about anything."

The next step is to find how best to make this policy truly effective. The International Harvester program, which with some variations is used by many organizations, makes regular use of three means of communication with factory employees:

1. *The Weekly News Letter,* distributed to all members of the management group. This includes supervisors in both shop and office. It is not confidential, and it is expected that supervisors will pass on the information in it to their employees.

2. *The Managerial Bulletin*, which is like a newspaper extra. It appears at no regular interval. There might be three issues in one day, and then no other issue for weeks. The purpose is to give all supervisors news while it is news, so that when any employee hears a rumor he will know from experience that he can go to his supervisor and get the facts. It is an effective rumor killer. And, too, it brings about a closer relationship between the supervisor and those who work under his supervision. It is highly desirable for employees to feel that their supervisors are the ones to whom they should go for reliable information about any phase of their working conditions. Unless management gives adequate information to the supervisors, *and promptly*, employees will depend on other and often unreliable sources for their information. The morale of both the supervisor and his employees will suffer.

3. *Letters from the Works Manager*, sent straight to the homes of all employees when it is important that all employees be told the same facts at the same time, and especially when it is desirable that the families of employees know the story too.

THE EMPLOYEE MAGAZINE

More than four thousand employee magazines are published at an estimated cost of about seventy million dollars a year. Much of this expenditure is wasted because adequate advance thought was not given to deciding just what the purpose of the magazine should be and what editorial policy would best accomplish that purpose.

The statement of purpose and editorial policy of one employee magazine is given below:

Purpose. The purpose of the ____________ is to help all of the people in the organization—executive and nonexecutive, office and shop—to become better acquainted with each other, because when people get to know each other better a happy and harmonious working relationship is so much easier to achieve.

Editorial Policy. People are interested in news, especially news with a human interest element. Feature articles about unusual things employees are doing, with shorter news stories about weddings, graduations, outings, contests won, and so on (with plenty of pictures), will make up the bulk of the material. But gossip of the type which will embarrass anyone will never knowingly be published.

There will be items which will be of special interest to the families of employees.

Company news will be included, but it can and should be made interesting. Often the story of a new product, for example, has in it real human interest possibilities.

An occasional serious statement of why the management believes a certain action to be necessary is not out of place—if it does not try to preach.

Employees are interested in financial facts about the company, if these facts are stated frankly, openly, and truthfully and not in technical "balance-sheet" language.

Suggested Supplementary Reading on Two-Way Communication

Communication Within Industry, Raymond W. Peters.

The material for this book was gathered during an extensive study of employer-employee communication conducted by the author for the Esso Standard Oil Company with the purpose of improving that company's program. Each of the various methods of communication is discussed in a separate chapter. In the final chapter there is a summary and statement of conclusions.

Handbook of Personnel Management, George D. Halsey.

Chapter XX, Two-Way Communication.

The Art of Readable Writing, Rudolf Flesch.

This book presents Dr. Flesch's famous "readability formula" and contains many suggestions which will be of great value to anyone who writes and wants other people to read and understand what he has written.

CHAPTER XIX

The Work of the Employee Counselor

"EMPLOYEE counselor" is a comparatively new title in personnel supervision although the functions performed by the counselors are not new.

To fulfill production schedules caused by the demands of World War II, manufacturing plants throughout the country found it necessary to expand their working forces enormously. The supply of experienced workers of all kinds was soon exhausted and large numbers of inexperienced workers were brought in, many of them being women who had never done production work before. Newly appointed supervisors, and even the "old-timers" in many shops, found the supervision of women an entirely new experience. Also, in most cases the product was different, necessitating many changes in machinery and tools and requiring the foremen to give the major share of their time to problems which had to do with mechanical and technical matters.

But the new employees had many personal problems which were pressing, such as, finding living quarters, someone to take care of the children while they were at work, transportation to and from work. And, if they could not find satisfactory solutions to these problems, they quit and went somewhere else or, if they stayed, were not able to do their best work. Gradually, those who could and would help with these problems found themselves doing more and more of this type of work and so, quite informally, they became "employee counselors."

"It is evident that the developments in employee counseling in war industries have been influenced principally by emergency needs and the extent to which they could or could not be met by the established personnel and line organization, and to a much lesser degree by previous counseling experiments in industry or by the growth of counseling in nonindustrial fields. It is also apparent, however, that counseling is introducing into personnel work in many companies a new emphasis on the value of helping the individual meet personal problems which interfere with his satisfactory adjustment to the job."[1]

Duties of Employee Counselors

1. *Helping the New Employee to become Oriented to the Job*

"In most companies counselors take an important part in the induction of new workers, particularly new women workers. First days at a plant are bewildering, and a counselor can do much to help housewives and office workers bridge the gap between their homes and offices and a noisy factory. Almost daily at Eastern Aircraft Division of General Motors Corporation, a group of fledgling riveters, welders, inspectors, and machine operators receive their industrial welcome from one of the counselors. She tells the women about the Wildcat planes they will be building, where they will be used, and who flies them. She tells about some of the procedures of production and the urgent necessity of meeting and passing production schedules. She explains company policies and rules, and with the aid of pamphlets she outlines the advantages of the company's Group insurance and hospitalization plan and the urgency of subscribing to the voluntary system of payroll deductions for war bond purchases. She tells the new women about her own job as counselor and how she is ready to help them with their problems.

"Then she introduces them to the plant. She takes them to the locker room, assigns them individual lockers, and teaches each one how to use a coat chain. She explains in detail the mysteries of timecards, how to ring in and out, how to use transfer cards on job changes and when promotions occur, and how to conform with plant security rules. She takes them on a tour of the cafeteria and gives them the list of meal hours. She tells them how and when to use the first-aid station."[2]

[1] From *Employee Counseling*, Helen Baker (published by the Industrial Relations Section, Princeton University).

[2] From *The Employee Counselor in Industry*, a report prepared by the Policyholders Bureau of the Metropolitan Life Insurance Co.

2. *Information and Assistance on Personal Problems Not Directly Connected with the Job.*

The counselor usually finds out, also, if there are any personal problems such as housing, transportation, or care of young children, and arranges to give help on these problems. The counselor tries to leave the new employee with the feeling "Here is a friend to whom I can come with problems which are too small or too personal to worry the foreman with."

"Increased hours of work, new jobs, migration to new and crowded communities, and rationing requirements have complicated greatly the lives of many industrial workers. When these complications result in a serious wastage of man-hours, they become of concern to management as well as to the employee. Almost every reporting company stated that the counseling service is expected to ascertain employee needs and to marshal information on in-company and community facilities planned to meet them.

"The extent of other in-company sources of help influences the types of information and other assistance for which the counselor is responsible. For example, information on medical care beyond the scope of the company's medical service may be provided by the industrial physician or nurse, and the counselor directs employees needing such help to the medical department. Similarly, if the company offers free legal consultation, the counselor may help the employee arrange for an appointment. The problem of the care of children of working mothers has become so acute that some companies have assigned this matter to a special counselor or have set up a new section in the personnel department to counsel with employees on child care facilities. Considerable emphasis is given to the importance of close cooperation between the counseling staff and those in-company specialized services to which counselors may refer employees.

"Except in the few companies in which special child care counseling is provided, women counselors usually develop a file of information on day nurseries, summer camps, and other arrangements for the supervision of children of pre-school and school age, and work closely with community counseling and child-care agencies. Information on housing is another important service given by counselors. In some of the federal agencies, such information is made available through counseling interviews before the individual starts work so that the worker may become settled in the community as quickly as possible. A number of counselors report that they provide information on recreational, social, religious, and educational facilities. These services are useful in promoting stability by helping the worker find normal satisfaction in the war-time community."[3]

3. *Listening to and Discussing Personal Problems and Difficulties Connected with the Job*

This is the most difficult, the most fraught with danger, and yet the richest in possibilities of service to the employee and to the management of any of the counselor's duties.

"Variously characterized as the 'understanding ear,' the 'patient, understanding friend,' and the 'listening post' function, this aspect of the counselor's job is given a major emphasis by many companies. This function is to some extent an indivisible part of the job of supervision, but, engrossed in production problems, wartime supervisors are likely to have little time to listen to employee grievances or problems. Moreover, many employees hesitate to thrust their personal difficulties upon an immediate supervisor. Where counselors are provided, and not burdened with too many other responsibilities, the employee is encouraged and given the direct opportunity to discuss freely his attitudes and problems with someone who has time to listen, and who will not use the information in any way that will endanger the employee's self-respect or his status in the organization.

"Under some programs, the employee may discuss anything with the counselor. In other cases, announcements concerning the counseling service state specifically or imply that personal problems brought up should have some relation to the job situation. While the counseling service gives the employee a chance to discuss certain job difficulties which he might not be willing to discuss with the foreman, emphasis is usually given to the importance of leaving all decision making to the foreman, in order to avoid weakening the supervisor's status. A number of companies find that women counselors are particularly helpful in

[3] From *Employee Counseling*, by Helen Baker.

getting to the bottom of problems among girls and women that would never come to light if left to male foremen."[4]

In all counseling, but in this phase especially, the interview should be on friendly, confidential, nonauthoritative basis. Some organizations have given the counselors authority for the enforcement of certain rules, even for administering discipline. The consensus seems to be that this is undesirable for two reasons. First, the employee is much less likely to talk freely about his attitudes to someone who has disciplinary authority. Second, it is likely to confuse the employee to some extent as to exactly who is his boss. The employee is directly responsible to his supervisor in all matters, and there should be nothing in organization or administration which causes any confusion in the employee's mind with respect to this.

The counselor is, and should always remain, just a friend who is well informed as to company policy and company and community services and who stands ready to give any help and advice needed; *but who has no supervisory authority* of any kind.

Such a counselor can be of great assistance to the employee, to the supervisor, and to management.

Suggested Supplementary Reading on the Work of the Employee Counselor

Employee Counseling, Helen Baker.

This is an exceptionally well written report of a study of the experiences of some sixty or more organizations with employee counseling. The author is associate director of the Industrial Relations Section of Princeton University.

The Employee Counselor in Industry, a report prepared by the Policyholder's Service Bureau of the Metropolitan Life Insurance Co.

This report summarizes the experience of twenty-eight companies and the War Department.

The Woman Counselor in Industry, Dorothy K. Newman.

This is a Special Bulletin (#16) of the Woman's Bureau of the U.S. Department of Labor. It describes several plans, with especial emphasis on plans used in shipyards.

[4] From Employee Counseling, Helen Baker.

Empoylee Counseling: A New Personnel Assignment," Ordway Tead.

This article, in the July-September, 1943, issue of *Advanced Management*, described the development of the idea, lists the duties of the counselor, and offers a tentative draft of a "code of standard practice."

CHAPTER XX

Improving Work Methods

Too often supervisors in shop and office consider the planning of improved methods of doing the work in their departments as being exclusively the responsibility of specialists "from the office"; but this is not the case. Improvement of work methods is and always has been an important part of the supervisor's job. It is true, however, that the man from the time-study or planning office can often suggest improvements which both the employee doing the job and you, his supervisor, have overlooked. There are two reasons for this, but both are due to conditions which you can correct.

First, there is the natural tendency to let closeness to the job and having done the thing a certain way for years blind you to possible improvements. This you can overcome by forming the habit of questioning everything and by refusing definitely to accept any method as being the *best* one just because the job has been done that way with reasonable success for years.

The second reason is that the man from the planning division approaches his task in a systematic manner. He applies a few fundamental principles of work organization and motion economy according to a well designed plan from which he seldom varies. But you can use the same plan and can apply the same principles. In other words, there is nothing in the way of knowledge or equipment that the time-study man has which it is not readily possible for you also to have. And you have the added advantage of knowing both the job and the worker better than the "man from the office" can know them. And this is a real advantage.

A Six-Step Plan for Studying and Improving Work Methods

Step I: Prepare in writing a detailed, step-by-step description of exactly how the job is being done now

Familiar as you are with how each job in your section is done, it might seem that it would not be necessary for you to write down the description in full detail, but such is not the case. There is something about writing down each small thing done which makes those things which are unnecessary stand out like "sore thumbs."

For example, you probably shave practically every morning. You should be fully familiar with what you do and certainly should have reduced the process to the least possible number of motions. But write down exactly what you do with each hand during each step of the process and, unless you are much more efficient than I was, you will find that from 15 to 20 per cent of the motions are unnecessary and that you are doing almost everything with one hand while the other is idle. And you will probably never realize this unless you do prepare such a complete written job "breakdown" (as this type of job description is usually called).

Women supervisors will probably find that a similar breakdown of the morning task of applying cream, powder, lipstick, etc., will show that they are no more efficient in this than are the men in shaving.

When preparing the breakdown of a job to be studied use one line for each small thing which is done. Any grouping of several details will make study more difficult. For example, in describing how a workman obtains his material for assembling a certain device it might seem sufficient to say:

1. Gets twelve strips of metal, and six strips of insulation from an adjacent table.

But study and elimination of unnecessary motions will be greatly facilitated by describing this part of the operation in about the following manner:

(1) Gets up from seat at workbench.
(2) Walks to supply table, ten feet away.

(3) Counts twelve strips of metal (size 2″ by 10″) using both hands.
(4) Places strips on table.
(5) Counts six strips of insulating material, using both hands, ending with strips in left hand.
(6) Picks up metal strips with right hand.
(7) Walks back to work bench—ten feet.
(8) Places metal and insulation strips on work bench immediately in front of seat, metal to his left.
(9) Sits down at bench.

It might even be desirable to break down steps 3 and 5 more fully. This will be done in a later analysis, unless these steps are to be eliminated.

Such a detailed breakdown may seem foolish at first glance, but only by such method is the attention focussed on those details which can be eliminated. For example, it might be found that the operator does need the strips of metal and insulation and that the number taken is the best number for him to have in easy reach on his bench. But, even so, four details in the breakdown stand out—(1) Gets up; (2) Walks; (7) Walks; (9) Sits down—and, since these are all obviously nonproductive and time-consuming acts, serious thought will be given as to how they can be eliminated. If they were not actually written down they might easily be overlooked.

The breakdown should be written on a simple form, which may easily be prepared by the supervisor. It is just a sheet of paper headed as shown below.

Operation ____________________ Date ____________________

Job Name ____________________ Operator(s) ____________________

No. *Details of Present Method* *Action Suggested*

It is desirable to complete this description of how each detail of the entire job is handled before any attempt is made to improve the methods used. As you write the descriptions you will probably see possible improvements. If you stop to work these out, you may get just that far and no farther. Complete the description of the present method first, *then* take the next step, which is:

Step II: Question every detail

These questions should be asked concerning each separate detail of the breakdown.

1. WHY is this detail performed? What purpose does it accomplish, and is this purpose a necessary one? If it is necessary, can the same purpose be accomplished without the performance of this detail?
2. WHO should do this part of the job? WHERE should it be done? WHEN should it be done? Can it be done more economically and just as satisfactorily by some one else and can he do it better at some other time and place?
3. HOW should it be done? Can the present method be improved upon? Are there unnecessary or needlessly difficult and awkward motions? Are all materials and tools in the places where they can be most easily reached by the operator? Are they so placed that he picks them up naturally in the position in which they will be used?

Practice has shown that the best method is first to ask the "why" questions concerning *all of the details*, before asking the other questions. The purpose of asking these questions first is to determine what details may be eliminated. When it looks as if any detail can be eliminated, write "E" in the column headed "Action Suggested." For instance, in the example given, we might reasonably expect to eliminate details 1, 2, 7, and 9. Certainly it must be possible to get the material to the worker's bench in a way which will not require this getting up and walking. "E" will, therefore, be written after these details.

Next, "who, where, and when" should be asked concerning each step. If a carefully considered answer to any question makes some change in method seem desirable, a brief note describing the proposed change should be put in the column headed "Action Suggested" or on a separate sheet of paper. For example, it might be decided that it would be more economical to have a lower-paid employee in the stock room count the metal and insulation strips and place paper markers in the piles so the more skilled workman can pick up the proper number with each hand.

Finally, the "how" questions are asked in an endeavor to find the best way to do each necessary detail.

The "best" way is the one in which unnecessary details are eliminated, and the motions to carry out the necessary details are so planned that the work is easier and less fatiguing. To find this best way of doing any detail of the job requires the application of certain principles of motion economy. Barnes suggests the following:

1. Motions of the two hands should be simultaneous and symmetrical.
2. Tools and materials should be located close in and directly in front of the operator so as to be within easy reach of the hands. Transport distances should be as short as possible and movements should be as few as possible.
3. There should be a definite and fixed place for all tools and materials.
4. Gravity feed bins and containers should be used to deliver materials close to the point of use.
5. Tools and materials should be pre-positioned wherever possible.
6. "Drop deliveries" should be used wherever possible.
7. The hands should be relieved of all work that can be done more advantageously by the feet. Power-operated tools and equipment should be used wherever economical. A vise, jig, or fixture should be used to hold the work wherever possible, this releasing the hands for productive work.
8. Materials and tools should be located to permit the best sequence of motions. Rhythm is essential to a smooth easy work pattern.
9. Smooth continuous motions of the hands are preferable to zigzag motions or straight-line motions involving sudden and sharp changes in direction.
10. The height of the work place and the chair should preferably be arranged to permit alternate sitting and standing at work. Adequate lighting should be provided, and the worker should be made as comfortable as possible.[1]

Step III: Work out and write a breakdown of the proposed new methods

From notes made in answering the questions, prepare a complete breakdown of the proposed new method. Then review this

[1] From *Work Methods Manual*, Ralph M. Barnes (John Wiley & Sons). The ten principles are discussed in considerable detail and each principle is illustrated by examples showing its application to actual cases.

quickly, asking the same questions to be sure your proposals will stand up.

Step IV: Secure permission to put the plan into operation

Present your suggestion to the executive to whom you report and secure his permission to put the plan into effect. Unless your department is on a wage incentive plan which will take care of the matter, decide and secure approval of what is right and fair in the way of salary increase for the operator if he increases his output.

You will, of course, give credit to whoever may have helped you in working out the improved method.

Step V: Explain the improved method to the workers affected

Many worth-while improvements have failed because they were put into effect without explaining them in advance to the persons who were affected by the changes. The operator and anyone who must handle differently either raw material or finished product should have the changes explained to them. The operator should know in advance, too, just what effect this will have on his earnings. If there is a union, the representative in the department should have the change explained to him.

Better still, is to have these people help in working out both the new method and new compensation plan. Then this important step will have been taken care of in advance.

Step VI: Put the improved method into operation

If all the steps prior to this have been taken care of carefully, the actual putting into operation will be a simple matter—but overconfidence is never wise. Watch the new operation most carefully at first to be sure everything is working as planned.

And be constantly on the lookout for further improvements.

Suggested Supplementary Reading on Improving Work Methods

Work Methods Manual, Ralph M. Barnes.

A practical book written especially for supervisors and workers on the principles of work organization and work economy. Each principle is illustrated with a description of how it was applied in an actual case. The chapter headings are: 1. Introduction; 2. Developing a Better Method; 3. The Job Breakdown; 4. Process Charts; 5. Activity Charts; 6. Operation Analysis; 7. Fundamental Hand Motions; 8. and 9. Ten Principles of Motion Economy; 10. Putting the New Method into Effect.

Time Study Fundamentals for Foremen, Phil Carroll, Jr.

"The purpose of this book is to give the practical foreman a working knowledge of the elementary principles involved in studying and measuring the time it takes to do a job."

"J.M.T." Course, prepared by the Training-Within-Industry Division of the War Manpower Commission.

A short course (five two-hour sessions) that summarizes the best thinking of many able men on the subject of improving work methods. Every supervisor who has an opportunity to do so should take this course.

The work of the Training-Within-Industry Division of the War Manpower Commission is being carried forward by the Training-Within-Industry Foundation, Summit, New Jersey (a nonprofit organization).

CHAPTER XXI

Wage Incentive Plans

WHAT is the ideal wage plan?

This question has had an important place on almost every program of meetings of executives of shops, offices, or stores since the days of Frederick W. Taylor. But too often the search has been for some incentive plan which, when installed, will *immediately* solve all the problems of supervision and management by *automatically* causing the employees to work harder and more efficiently, making them happy on their jobs, and increasing the profits of the business. The executive of today probably has no more chance of finding a wage incentive plan which will *by itself* do all of these things than had the alchemists of finding something which would turn lead into gold.

No wage incentive payment plan, no matter how carefully and intelligently designed, will work effectively unless it is well administered. It is a tool, and even a good tool poorly handled is likely to do more harm than good. But like any other good tool in the hands of a capable workman, a good wage incentive plan, skillfully and sympathetically administered, will accomplish much.

ESSENTIALS OF A GOOD WAGE INCENTIVE PLAN[1]

Fair to worker and management. An important requirement for lasting success of any wage incentive plan is that it shall be fair to

[1] This list of essentials is made up by combining five such lists from the following sources: *Wage Incentive Methods*, Charles W. Lytle (Ronald Press); *Human Nature and Management*, Ordway Tead (McGraw-Hill Book Co.); "Trends in Incentive Compensation," a speech by J. W. Nicherson, reported in American Management Production Series #150 (1944); "Essentials in Incentive Compensation," a speech by John W. Riegel, reported in American Management Personnel Series #77 (1944); and *How to Be a Leader*, George D. Halsey (Harper & Brothers).

both worker and management in every detail of its design and administration. If any feature cannot stand impartial judgment as to its fairness, then that part must be changed or the plan will not live. The worker must not have his earnings penalized for anything beyond his control, such as poor quality material which slows down his production, experimental or development work, or requests to leave his machine (or to leave the selling floor, if a salesperson) more than the normal time, unless allowance is made which compensates him fairly for production time lost.

On the other hand, the management, too, must be treated fairly. No plan is quite fair which increases earnings, but does not at the same time increase production. Nor can the management be asked to guarantee minimum annual earnings or even a minimum daily wage and be expected to give the worker all of the extra he earns when he exceeds standard production.

Major encouragement on most important factor. Perhaps the first step in the design of a wage incentive plan should be to decide just what are the relative importances of the various parts of the employee's job effort—just what shall be emphasized most. In shops the parts usually considered are quantity of work, quality of work, and economy in the use of materials. Most plans emphasize quantity of work, but it is quite possible that there are conditions in which either of the other two might deserve the major emphasis. In retail stores the four parts might be sales volume, accuracy in store system, stock keeping duties, customer good will. Many store executives do not like straight commission plans because too much of the incentive is on immediate sales volume.

Encourage well-rounded effort. The plan should, in some effective manner, encourage and reward parts of the employee's work other than the major part, including, for example, such important things in the work of a retail salesperson as efficiency in stock work, co-operation in keeping the buyer informed as to customer wants, courtesy in selling and in handling exchanges. The shop employee should be encouraged by the plan to keep up the quality of his output, and to use materials economically.

Reward proportional to individual effectiveness. Incentives applied to individuals are, as a rule, more effective than those applied to groups. In some cases, however, where small groups act as units and it is difficult to measure individual contribution, group incentive plans have been effective. Some larger group incentive plans have been effective also, but this is the exception rather than the rule.

Easily understood. The employee should be able to figure for himself, all along, just how he stands; just how much extra compensation he has earned. A complicated system may be fair, but it is doubtful if the person who gets no extra compensation will think so.

Steady earnings. The week-to-week, month-to-month fluctuations in earnings should not be too large, and this is especially true if the fluctuations are caused by things outside the employees' control, such as poor material to work with, weather, sudden change in fashion.

All earn. The plan should be such that, if there is extra compensation in the form of bonus, premium, or commission, a fairly large proportion of all employees (probably at least two-thirds) should regularly earn some of this extra compensation. Any plan in which only a few earn anything above their weekly wage is usually considered unfair by those who do not earn it.

Standards carefully set, then not changed. It is most important that the standard by which the amount of incentive payment is to be determined shall be most carefully set, using all available scientific aids. Many of the earlier incentive plans used the average of previous output in setting piece rates and, when the workers greatly increased their production, these piece rates were cut. Management said the workers had been loafing; workers said the whole plan was just a ruse to get them to do more work for the same money.

Substantial total earnings possible. The rates should be so set that a good worker can, with reasonable effort, earn appreciably more than the market rate in the locality for his type of work.

Indirect workers included. If possible some way should be found to bring all workers into the plan. The trucker, the tool boy, and the sweeper all work better if they feel that their work is recognized as contributing to the success of the department as a whole.

Supervisors included. The supervisor is to a large degree, responsible for the efficiency of his entire section, and increased effort and effectiveness on his part should be rewarded promptly by an increase in his pay check. Any wage incentive plan which does not include the supervisor has a serious weakness.

Good administration. There is probably no one thing more essential to the success of any wage incentive plan than that there shall be continuous, intelligent, and sympathetic supervision by management of every phase of its operation. The supervisor plays an important part in this. It is his responsibility, first to see that every employee in his section understands the plan, and second, to make sure that all cases where employees are entitled to "allowances" for slowdowns in production caused by things beyond their control are reported promptly, and adjustments made. There is a big advantage if this can be done without it being necessary for the employee to ask for the allowance.

Employees have a part in design and administration. More and more it is becoming a practice of management to ask employee representatives to sit with management representatives when such important personnel matters as wage incentive plans are being decided upon. This makes selling the plan to the rank and file employees a much simpler matter.

Employees, through their representatives, should have an active part in the administration of the plan, especially in discussing such questions as how much a change in manufacturing practices should change a standard time, or how much a change in demand due to a change in fashion should change a commission rate. If all of these matters are explained in advance, there will be little friction.

SUGGESTED SUPPLEMENTARY READING ON WAGE INCENTIVE PLANS

Wage Incentive Methods, Charles W. Lytle.
A painstaking and thorough description and analysis of a large number of wage incentive plans.

Personnel Management, Scott, Clothier, and Spiegel.
Chapter XXIV, Wage Payment Plans.

Human Nature and Management, Ordway Tead.
On pages 260 and 261 there is a brief summary of four "psychological considerations which arise to affect the value of incentives, particularly for the rank and file."

Timestudy Fundamentals for Foremen, Phil Carroll, Jr.
Chapter II, Incentive Plans Explained.

CHAPTER XXII

The Supervisor's Part in the Prevention of Accidents

Bill Schulz was foreman of the grinder department in a large machine shop. The buffing wheel occasionally jerked small parts out of the hands of the operator and these went immediately to the space below the blades of the exhaust fan. Bill always told every new man to shut down the fan and to be absolutely sure it had stopped before reaching in for a part. But this shut down about half the department for a few moments as the men could not grind while the exhaust fan was shut down. So Bill, knowing exactly the clearance between the blades and the bottom of the drum occasionally reached in and got small parts with the fan running.

It was perfectly safe for him to do this because he knew exactly what he was doing.

Charlie Brown was a new man. He had been told about the necessity of shutting down the fan; but, also, he had seen Bill reach in for small parts two or three times. One day the buffer jerked a small part from Charlie's hands. Bill had stepped out of the department for a few moments, but Charlie felt that he knew exactly how Bill had reached into the drum, so he tried it. He lost two fingers and was absent from work for several weeks.

Bill Schulz now realizes that for the foreman to tell his men to do one thing and to do differently himself does not make a safe department.

In another shop we found it difficult to prevent the machine operators from wearing four-in-hand ties or other things which could catch in the machines. The shop superintendent, who never operated a machine and therefore could safely wear any tie he wanted to, started wearing a bow tie and urged every foreman to do the same. Soon the problem was solved. "Do-as-I-do" had won where "do-as-I-say" had failed.

Careful analysis of the accident records in many shops has shown that about three-fourths of all accidents are due to "human causes," to carelessness or ignorance of the operator, to a desire to show off, to practical jokes and other forms of "horseplay," to absent-mindedness or thoughtlessness. All these conditions are corrected, not primarily by better safety devices, although these are most essential, *but by better supervision.*

The Bell Telephone System has adopted this slogan:

> No job is so important and no service so urgent that
> we cannot take time to perform our work safely.

Some Things the Supervisor Can Do to Promote Safety

1. *Set a good example himself.* No one thing a supervisor can do will help more to make his department a safe department than for him to observe carefully all of the safety rules. If he is careful about such things as always wearing goggles when he grinds tools, taking proper care of any scratches or minor cuts he may receive, picking up any loose material some one might fall over, not making adjustments while machines are in motion unless it is safe for a less experienced man to do so, he will have gone a long way toward having a safe department.

2. *Emphasize the importance of safety when teaching new employees.* Instruction in safe methods should be an important part of training of every new employee. If this instruction is assigned to one of the experienced workmen, the supervisor should check to be sure safety instruction is being given *and that the instructor is setting a good example in safe practices.*

3. *Make certain that tools and equipment are in good condition.* New men do not know the dangers to themselves and others of using faulty equipment such as chisels with mushroomed heads, poor clamps which occasionally allow cutting tools to slip. And experienced men are often careless about such things. It is the supervisor's responsibility to see that all of his equipment is both safe and efficient, and that safety devices really work.

4. *Be on the alert for and correct unsafe practices.* The super-

visor should *know* the safe way to do each thing in his department and when he sees anything being done in a manner which is unsafe he should show the person the better way and explain why. He should see that there are no pranks or horseplay, especially in departments where accidents may be caused. Regularity and persistence in this practice are important.

5. *Look for and report any need for safety devices and guards.* All safety men know that careful workmen are more important than guards and safety devices, but that these are important. Every supervisor should be constantly on the lookout for devices which may be installed to make it harder to get hurt in his department.

6. *Keep stairways and aisles clean and clear.* Many accidents are caused by bits of wood or metal or possibly some oil in the aisle or on a stairway. He should watch especially for anything which may project from a pile of material and catch on clothing or passing trucks.

7. *Learn first aid, and be prepared to assist.* Every supervisor should learn something about first aid, at least how to handle an injured person until help can get there. He should know exactly where and how to call for help.

8. *Try to help the employee who seems worried.* An employee who is worried about conditions at home, his personal finances, his security in his position, or anything else is much more likely to have accidents than one who is not worried. If one of your employees appears to be worrying about something, try tactfully to find out what is causing the anxiety and see if you cannot do something to help eliminate the cause. Suggestions on how this may be done are given in Chapter XIV.

9. *Prepare accident and compensation reports promptly and fully.* This may not help to prevent accidents, but it will help the man who has been hurt to secure more promptly any compensation to which he is entitled.

Suggested Supplementary Reading on Prevention of Accidents

How to Train Supervisors, R. D. Beckman.
Discussion Outlines 6 and 7 deal with accident prevention.

Handbook of Personnel Management, George D. Halsey.
Chapter XXII, Prevention of Accidents.

Industrial Safety Guide, National Safety Council.
This booklet, which is revised frequently, gives the latest thinking of the Safety Council on accident prevention.

Industrial Supervisor, a magazine published monthly by the National Safety Council.

CHAPTER XXIII

Morale

What It Is and How It Is Created

Morale in a business or industrial organization is an attitude of emotional readiness which enables the worker to turn out more and better work without increase in fatigue; which causes him to enter enthusiastically into the activities and endeavors of the group with which he works; and which makes him less susceptible to outside influences, especially those which base their appeal on the premise that management's sole interest in him is to get all it can and give as little as possible in return.

It is purely emotional, in that it has to do entirely with how the worker *feels* about his job, his supervisor, and his company, rather than with the actual facts; yet the creating and maintaining of a high degree of morale in the group under his supervision is probably any executive's most important responsibility.

But, and this is most important, it cannot be bought or ordered or reasoned or even persuaded into existence.

It can be created only by introducing into the work situation of each member of the group certain conditions favorable to its development, and no person in the organization plays a larger part in this than the employee's direct supervisor.

First of all each worker must find some opportunity for self-expression in his work. He must be able to do his task well enough so that he has a feeling of pride in his performance. If, at first, he lacks skill and confidence, he must be given these by encouragement and training. The worker who does not know how to do his work really well, who does not have some margin of skill and knowledge over that which is needed barely to get by, will never get any satisfaction out of his job. His morale will be low. And, as his skill and knowledge increase, if he is to continue to get full satisfaction from his work, his supervisor should ask his advice and co-operation about any contemplated changes which will affect the worker. All of this adds to the worker's feeling of personal accomplishment, personal worth-whileness. He will then be able to compare himself with others about him and not feel ashamed.

Second, each must feel that his efforts are appreciated, that his supervisor and the management realize both the difficulty and the importance of what he is doing, that they do not in any way look down on him or his work even though this work may be of a somewhat routine character such, for example, as running an elevator. And as tangible evidence of this appreciation he must feel that he is fairly paid for what he does, especially that no one doing work which is no more difficult or important is paid more.

Third, he must believe in the worth-whileness of the general objectives of the organization and of his unit in the organization. It is said that prisoners required to carry a pile of brick from one side of the prison yard to the other and on alternate days carry them back will go crazy; while, if they were carrying the brick to build some worth-while structure, they would enjoy the work. Workers, especially young workers assigned to meaningless work (or work the meaning of which has not been explained to them, which amounts to the same thing), lose spirit and often quit to take jobs paying less.

Just as I reached this point in reading the rough draft of this chapter a young lady came into my office. She said that she wanted to apply for a position as stenographer. Inquiry developed that she was working with another organization and that her salary was somewhat higher than our beginning rate. But she wanted to come with us anyhow, and this was the reason she gave:

"I work for a finance company which makes small loans, largely to people who receive low salaries. The company charges two or three times the interest my father has to pay when he borrows at the bank. If a person cannot pay, we send hard-boiled letters and it is my job to write those letters. I just don't like that kind of business. I would be glad to work for less in order to change."

I do not know much about the company for which this young lady worked, but I understand that it is one of the better loan companies, charging no higher rate of interest than is made necessary by the type of loan handled. Probably it renders a worthwhile service to people who cannot get loans at commerical banks. But no one took the trouble to explain this to the stenographer who writes only to the borrowers who have caused trouble and knows nothing about the thousands who have really been helped. Her company may be serving a worthy purpose; but if she thinks the owners are just a bunch of loan sharks, the effect on her morale is the same as if they were all of that.

A feeling of at least a reasonable degree of pride in the aims, methods, and product of the company one works for is certainly a most important and probably an essential component of morale.

Fourth, there must be nothing required of the worker which will take away any of his feeling of self-respect, which will prevent him from maintaining that simple, human dignity which everyone desires. Arbitrary orders without explanation, criticism in front of others, rules or practices that seem to imply suspicion as to one's honesty—all these and similar things take something away from a person's self-respect and build up a resentment against management. This is bad for morale. Sometimes strict rules of this type are necessary. Two simple precautions will prevent resentment. The first is to explain why the rule is necessary and the second is to make the rule as nearly as universal in its application as possible. The workman will not resent inspection of packages he takes out, for example, if his foreman is willing to have the packages he takes out inspected.

Fifth, the worker must be reasonably free from worry. Most important in the elimination of worry is a feeling of security, a feeling that the job is at least reasonably permanent and secure; that if reductions must be made they will be made on carefully considered merit, and that the person being laid off will be given all possible notice and help in his efforts to find another job. There must, also, be the knowledge that, should unexpected and unusual emergencies arise, ways are provided by the management or some employee organization so that he can get whatever help he may need—medical care, legal or general advice, or financial aid.

Sixth, each worker must feel that there is ahead of him opportunity for advancement, and that promotions are made on the basis of merit only.

Seventh, he must like personally and respect the ability of his supervisor. Above all he must feel that his supervisor is fair and that there are no favorites who receive special consideration.

Eighth, and last, he must find in the work environment a satisfying social experience.

If these eight conditions exist in the thinking and feeling of the employees of any group, morale will be high, and just to the extent that they do not exist, will it be found that the morale is not what it should be.

Check your own department carefully on each of the eight conditions.

Supplementary Reading on Morale

Management and the Worker, Roethlisberger and Dickson.

The book describes a study of factory workers extending over a period of years which showed that factors other than physical working conditions seem to have greater effect on output than do physical working conditions.

Human Nature and Management, Ordway Tead.

Chapter XIII, The Creation of Morale.

Handbook of Personnel Management, George D. Halsey.

Chapter I, Objectives and Guiding Principles of Sound Personnel Management.

CHAPTER XXIV

The N.A.F. Code of Ethics for Foremen[1]

1. The Foreman should recognize that every man above, beside or below, has an inherent desire to do good work and to be a useful and respected citizen. Until he has considered every possible motive, he should not assume that any man wants to do anything less than his best.

2. The Foreman should keep an open mind on all subjects, and strive to maintain a broad and balanced outlook. He should always be willing to recognize merit in another's ideas.

3. The Foreman should deal fairly with all his associates in the company. Being in an important position, he should assume responsibility for his own mistakes and refrain from shifting blame to others.

4. The Foreman should strive to understand the principles of business which make for the success or failure of industry. He should pass on to his men all the fundamentals of business principles so they can see, for themselves, their own relation to the general scheme.

5. The Foreman should keep informed as to the latest development in equipment and processes. He should recommend or put into effect such methods as will produce improved quality and lower costs for his products, and improve working conditions.

6. The Foreman must feel that one phase of his profession is to help working people obtain maximum satisfaction from life.

7. The Foreman should endeavor to earn, and carefully guard, a reputation for good moral character, good citizenship and common honesty; and he should support and promote all the uplifting influences of the community.

[1] This code of ethics is reprinted here with the permission of the National Association of Foremen, the copyright owners.

CHAPTER XXV

A Suggested Program For Your Development in the Art of Supervising People

---

THIS is the most important chapter in the book.

The ability really to supervise people; to be able to take a group of ordinary folk plugging along in a halfhearted way at their daily grind of work and to make out of that group a capable and enthusiastic team, getting more pay and more pleasure out of the job and giving more in service than they ever have before; to be able to see possibilities in a person who is just on the edge of failure, to search for and discover the thing which is holding him back—whether it be lack of courage, inadequate knowledge, or just a need for better direction of his energies—and, somehow, to furnish what is lacking and guide him skillfully from failure to success; that ability can bring to you more in success as it is usually measured and more in the deeper, richer satisfactions of life than can any other ability you may possess.

Undoubtedly, you now have a fair measure of this ability. You are interested in people and in methods of helping people or, long since, you would have put this book aside. You have, too, a desire to improve that natural aptitude for supervising people you now have—or, again, the book would never have been read to this point.

With this interest in people and this desire to improve your skill in helping them, you have travelled a long way on the road toward achievement of the best in the art of supervising people. The only thing that remains is for you to make a definite plan for building up of any places where you may be weak, and then to follow that plan thoughtfully, conscientiously and persistently.

The first step is to prepare carefully the self-rating which follows:

Rating on Personal Qualities Important to Success in Supervising People

The major headings of the rating are the six personal qualities given in Chapter II as being important to success in supervising people. Under each heading are several questions to help you to decide to what extent you possess that quality.

Answer each question by writing in the space provided a number which will indicate your carefully considered opinion of the extent to which you do the things described in the question. Use the following scale:

5. Excellent, probably better than about nine out of ten people you know.
4. Very good, probably better than about three-fourths of the people you know.
3. About equal to the average of the people you know.
2. Rather weak, probably six or seven out of ten people you know are better.
1. Seriously deficient, probably eight or nine out of ten people you know are better.

Try to be as impersonal as possible in this rating of yourself. Review the evidence just as though "yourself" were another person. Rate on the basis of what you have actually done, not what you believe you would do under different circumstances. The examples of behavior on which you base your judgments need not have been in connection with the actual supervision of people. What you do or have done at home, in school, or in club and church work is just as important in indicating the degree to which you possess the basic qualities necessary to success in supervising people as is what you do on the job while supervising people.

As you rate yourself, remember and take into account the tendency all of us are likely to have to rationalize our weaknesses in handling people. But, on the other hand, do not be too hard on yourself. Be as fair with yourself on the good side as on the bad side. This self-rating has only one purpose, to help you to develop a higher degree of skill in supervising people. It must show the true picture, good and bad, if it is to be of any real value to you.

When you finish answering the questions under the first heading, consider these answers carefully and rate yourself on *Thoroughness*. The rating will probably be not far from the average of your answers to the questions.

Continue in the same manner and rate yourself on the remaining qualities.

Thoroughness

To what extent do you usually plan in advance all of the details of any important project you undertake? ____4____

How conscientiously do you follow the plan after it is made? ____4____

How regularly do you stop just a second or two before you start even a small undertaking (such as making a minor repair on a plumbing fixture) and ask, "Do I have with me everything I will need?" ____5____

To what extent do you usually carry through to completion the projects you start? Consider all things you have started such as home study courses, home garden, keeping a diary, planning an improvement in your department, etc.? ____4____

How adequate is your system of making sure that you are reminded of duties and engagements and of promises you have made to do something like considering a raise for some employee at a given date, etc.? ____5____

How closely do you follow up on all details of the operation of your department to be sure nothing which should be done is overlooked? ____4____

How systematic and thorough are you in seeing that new employees are given all the information and assistance they need to help them to become happy and capable workers? ____4____

Look back over the mistakes you have made and the failures to accomplish what you have set out to do. Have these mistakes and failures often been caused primarily by lack of thoroughness on your part? If so, rate yourself low on this question. ____4____

After considering carefully your answers to all of the questions above, rate yourself on *Thoroughness*. [4.2]

4

Fairness

How careful are you to avoid making snap judgments about people and acting on these judgments?

How careful are you to avoid making promises to employees when you do not have authority to keep the promises?

When you do make a promise to do something for a person, how particular are you always to keep the promise?

How careful are you to avoid making careless remarks about people which may do them an injustice?

How careful, thorough, and conscientious are you in preparing "ratings" of your employees, or making recommendations for promotions?

How careful are you always to give credit to the proper person when your chief notices something in your department and commends you for it?

How careful are you to get the facts before you form an opinion about responsibility for an error?

To what extent do you make all reasonable effort to see that your employees have proper equipment and light so that they can do good work?

When you have made some comment about an employee which would tend to lower another person's opinion of him and you later find you were in error, how careful are you always to go to the person to whom you have spoken and correct your error?

Do you often thoughtlessly blurt out criticism either to or about a person without giving proper thought as to whether or not the criticism is fair? If so, rate yourself low on this question.

How careful are you to avoid showing your personal likes and dislikes of persons in your department?

After considering carefully your answers to the questions above, rate yourself on *Fairness*.

Initiative

To what extent are you resourceful in thinking of and suggesting new and effective means to accomplish any desired purpose?

When you are with a group of friends and the question arises as to what is to be done about the evening's entertainment, what to send a sick friend, how to pack something for overseas shipment or some similar matter, to what extent does the group usually listen to and follow your advice? 5

To what extent do you always notice and try to find out the reasons for or purposes served by such things as new and strange looking devices on electric light poles on your street, no visible marks on your laundry, an unusual tool or fixture in a shop you are visiting, the signal lights on the subway, changes in bus drivers on a trip, salesperson putting half the price ticket in a box when you buy a hat? 5

To what extent are you usually quick and positive in your decisions? 4

To what degree do you have faith in your own ability to supervise successfully a group of people doing a type of work with which you are familiar? 5

To what extent do you have courage, after a failure, to admit your part of the mistake and to try again? 5

How do you rate yourself when compared with other supervisors in the number of suggestions you make to your chief for improvement in your department? 5

How successful have you been in improving work methods in your department? 5

After considering carefully your answers to the questions above, rate yourself on *Initiative*. 39

Tact

How regularly do you remember to tell people about things you have read or heard that you know will please them, such as having seen in the paper that a son or daughter has won honors, or that you heard someone make a complimentary remark of some kind? 5

How do you rate yourself on how regularly and effectively you use the "praise technique" of supervision described on page 52? 5

How do you rate yourself on memory of names and faces? 3

How successful are you in always being able to think of the appropriate thing to say when unfortunate things have happened to people you know? 5

To what extent do your friends and employees come

to you to tell you of their personal difficulties and ask your advice and help? ________

To what extent do you make it a point to admit to the persons concerned that you have made a mistake when later developments show that you have been wrong in some opinion you have asserted quite strongly? ________

Co-operativeness may be defined as willingness and ability to work pleasantly with one's associates, always lending a helping hand when needed. How do you think your associates where you work would rate you on this quality? ________

Read again the rule on page 50. To what extent do you follow that rule? ________

To what extent do you refrain from following each story someone else tells about something he or a relative has done by telling a story of how you or someone you know has done even better? Think hard before you answer this one. It is a most common failing. ________

After considering carefully your answers to the questions above, rate yourself on *Tact*. [ ]

Enthusiasm

How successful have you been in getting other people enthusiastic about things in which you are interested? Include such things as organizing clubs, increasing attendance at Sunday School, getting people to subscribe to some worthy cause, personal selling of something like life insurance, getting your present employees enthusiastic about production goals or safety. ________

How strongly and deeply enthusiastic do you personally become about causes you believe to be important and worthy of support? ________

To what extent is your enthusiasm of the steady, lasting type rather than the type which "blows hot and cold"? ________

How do you think your associates, from just what they see of you every day, would rate you on enthusiasm? ________

After considering carefully your answers to the questions above, rate yourself on *Enthusiasm*. [ ]

Emotional Control

How regularly do you, before you speak, always consider the consequences of what you are about to say? ______

How fully are you able to keep from getting excited and acting unwisely in emergencies? ______

To what extent do you believe that your judgments about people are entirely free from influence of religious, social, or race prejudice? ______

How often has your temper or other emotional upset caused you to do or say things you later regretted? Include in this your relations with other members of your family and friends as well as with associates in business. Rate yourself low if your answer is "very often." ______

Are your feelings easily hurt? Rate yourself low if the answer is "Yes." ______

After you have made an important decision, how fully are you able to dismiss it from your mind and not worry about it? ______

When something happens to cause you embarrassment, how completely are you able to keep from worrying about it or brooding over it? ______

Can you take suggestions and instructions without becoming angry, even if not too tactfully given? ______

After considering carefully your answers to the questions above, rate yourself on *Emotional Control*. [ ]

Compute your *Total Rating* in the manner shown in the example below:

Rating on Thoroughness	3.5	× 5 =	17.5
Rating on Fairness	4.0	× 6 =	24.0
Rating on Initiative	2.5	× 5 =	12.5
Rating on Tact	4.5	× 4 =	18.0
Rating on Enthusiasm	3.0	× 2 =	6.0
Rating on Emotional Control	2.5	× 3 =	7.5
		25	
Sum			85.5
Rating (this sum divided by 25)			3.4

The choice of "weights" (numbers by which the original ratings are multiplied) is based on "votes" taken in many meetings of supervisors, but if you believe that, because of special conditions, different weights should be used, make any desired changes. The final rating will be the sum of the ratings after they are multiplied by the weights, divided by the sum of the weights.

But do not stop here. No matter how good your total score may be, you would, of course, like it to be better. And, for any large measure of success, you need a balanced development.

Choose for first attention, therefore, the quality on which you rated yourself the lowest. Read the chapters in this book and in the other books recommended, which offer suggestions, and make for yourself a definite written plan for improvement. Follow this plan conscientiously for a few weeks, then work on the quality which was next to the lowest. Continue in this manner on through the list—then start over again.

Self-improvement is a continuous, never-ending effort; but no other investment will pay you bigger dividends in success and happiness.

The Final Responsibility Is Yours

Finally, you must remember that the responsibility for your success or failure is primarily your own. As one chief executive said at a meeting of a group of his supervisors who had been discussing problems of personnel supervision:

"*Training is a sign post. It says that this or that is the right road, but you must walk the road yourself.*"

APPENDIX

A SUGGESTED LIBRARY ON SUPERVISION

For the person who wants, for his own bookshelf, a small library on supervising people, the first ten books on the list below are recommended. Where there is to be group discussion of the subject, all the books on the list should probably be in the library for reference purposes, with extra copies of the first ten available for lending to the members of the group.

The author will appreciate any suggestions of other books which readers of this book have found helpful.

Human Nature and Management, by Ordway Tead (New York: McGraw-Hill Book Co.; revised, 1933).

The first ten chapters present one of the best available explanations of those parts of psychology which are of the most interest to the business executive. The style is simple and straighforward, without any attempt to make it too "popular." Where psychological terms are used, they are adequately and simply defined.

The following chapters will be found to be especially interesting: III. The Inborn Tendencies to Action; IV. The Use and Control of Emotions; V. Forming and Changing Habits; VI. The Learning Process; VII. How to Encourage Reasoning; VIII. The Meaning of Will and Personality; IX. What are the Defense Mechanisms?

Management and the Worker, by F. J. Roethlisberger and William J. Dickson (Cambridge: Harvard University Press, 1939).

This book tells in considerable detail the story of one of the most interesting and extensive studies ever made of the "methods of dealing with employees." The study was made in the Hawthorne Plant of the Western Electric Company and extended over a period of about five years. It included studies of about 20,000 individual employees.

The Technique of Executive Control, by Erwin H. Schell (New York: McGraw-Hill Book Co.; 7th edition, 1950).

The chapter headings are: The Executive; Executive Attitude and Morale; Executive Tools; Executive Control; Executive Stimulation; Executive Duties; Executive Collaboration; Executive Public Relations; Difficulties with Subordinates; Difficulties with Associates; Difficulties with Superiors; Executive Improvement; Executive Proficiency; Executive Reading.

The questions and thought-provoking statements at the close of the discussion of each subject are especially helpful.

Training and Reference Manual for Job Analysis (Washington: Division of Occupational Analysis, U.S. Employment Service, 1946).

This manual is the outgrowth of eleven years of preparing job analyses in a wide variety of occupations and industries. It contains probably the most complete and detailed set of instructions available on how to prepare a job description and make a job analysis. Copies may be obtained from the Superintendent of Documents, U.S. Government Printing Office, Washington 25, D. C. Price 25 cents.

Job Evaluation, by Jay L. Otis and Richard H. Leukart (New York: Prentice-Hall, Inc., 1948).

The four basic systems of job evaluation (ranking, classification, point rating, and factor analysis) are described and examples given. The advantages and disadvantages of each system are discussed in detail.

Selecting and Inducting Employees, by George D. Halsey (New York: Harper & Brothers, 1951).

A list of the chapter headings follows: Vocationally Significant Qualities; Preparing the Job Specification; Recruiting Employees; The Application for Employment; Other Employment Office Procedures and Forms; The Physical Examination; Improving the Effectiveness of the Interview; Introducing and Developing a Testing Program; Selection and Validation of Tests; Tests of Mental Abilities; Tests of Manual Dexterity; Tests of Aptitude and Proficiency in Mechanical Trades; Tests of Aptitude and Proficiency in Office Occupations; Tests of Personality and Temperament; General Diagnostic Tests; Special Purpose Tests; "Home-Made" Tests; Five Successful Selection Programs; Special Selection Problems; Starting the New Worker on His Job.

Training Employees, by George D. Halsey (New York: Harper & Brothers, 1949).

The chapter headings are: Purpose and Importance of Training; General Teaching Principles Applied to Training; The Basic Training Pattern; The Conference as a Training Method; Guided Discussion; Other Training Methods and Devices; Use of Visual Aids in Training; Induction of New Employees and Information Booklets; How to Make Employee Meetings Interesting and Profitable; Training Industrial Workers; The Apprenticeship Plan for Skilled Workers; Training Office Workers; Training in Retail Stores; Training Outside

Salesmen; Training for Promotion; Fitting the College Graduate into the Organization; Improving Employee Attitudes; Training in Safety; Determining the Needs and Planning the Program; Measuring the Effectiveness of the Training Program.

Rating Employee and Supervisory Performance, edited by Joseph Dooher and Vivienne Marquis (New York: American Management Association, 1950).

This manual is made up of a selection of the best material AMA has published on the subject and, in addition, a specially prepared section based on AMA research.

Work Methods Manual, by Ralph M. Barnes (New York: John Wiley & Sons, 1944).

A short and intensely practical discussion of the principles of work organization and motion economy written especially for foremen and supervisors. Each principle and rule is illustrated by examples.

Handbook of Personnel Management, by George D. Halsey (New York: Harper & Brothers; revised edition, 1953).

A general book on personnel management written primarily for executives in factories, stores, and offices, and dealing especially with the practical aspects of the subject. The chapter headings are as follows: Objectives and Guiding Principles of Sound Personnel Management; Job Analysis; Preparing the Job Specification; Recruiting Employees; Employment Office Procedure and Forms; The Use of Tests as an Aid in Selecting Employees; Increasing the Effectiveness of the Employment Interview; Employment of Physically Impaired Persons; Induction of New Employees and Information Booklets; Training Employees—Objectives, Methods, and Principles; Some Typical Training Programs; Selection and Development of Supervisors; Employee Merit Rating; Correction and Discipline; Lay-offs and Dismissals; Job Evaluation and Salary Ranges; Wage-Incentive and Profit-Sharing Plans; Employment Stabilization and the Guaranteed Annual Wage; Special Considerations in the Employment and Supervision of Women; Two-Way Communication; Employee Grievances; Prevention of Accidents; Health, Recreation, and General Welfare; Group Insurance and Retirement; Collective Bargaining from Two Viewpoints; Examples of Labor-Management Co-operative Effort; The Foreman and the Union; Labor Relations in Non-Unionized Plants; Personnel Records and Statistics; Organization for Effective Personnel Management; Personnel Management in the Public Service; Outline for a Self-Audit of Personnel Management.

The Art of Leadership, by Ordway Tead (New York: McGraw-Hill Book Co., 1935).

Discusses interestingly the general qualities and methods of leadership.

The New Techniques for Supervisors and Foremen, by Albert Walton (New York: McGraw-Hill Book Co., 1940).

The author of this book was graduated as a mechanical engineer, and after twenty-five years in this field re-entered college and took his master and doctor's degrees in psychology. The result is an excellent, practical discussion of the applications of psychology to the problems of supervising people.

Handling Personality Adjustment in Industry, by Robert N. McMurry (New York: Harper & Brothers, 1944).

This book discusses some of the more pressing problems of personnel administration in the light of recent findings of psychology and psychiatry. Practical techniques for dealing with these problems are suggested.

How to Train Supervisors, by R. O. Beckman (New York: Harper & Brothers, 1940).

Part I describes in some detail the best methods of training supervisors through the means of "determinate discussion," which the author defines as "constructive discussion of which the scope is restrained and the direction pre-determined." Part II gives outlines for a supervisory training course of thirty-two meetings, using this method.

This is an invaluable book for leaders of groups discussing personnel supervision.

How to Interview, by Walter V. Bingham and Bruce V. Moore (New York: Harper & Brothers; 3rd revised edition, 1941).

This is a thorough discussion of the subject of interviewing.

The following chapters will be of especial interest: II. Learning How to Interview; VI. Interviewing Applicants for Employment; VII. Oral Examinations in Civil Service Agencies; IX. Interviewing Workers About Employer-Employee Relationships.

Interview Aids and Trade Questions for Employment Offices, by Lorin A. Thompson, Jr., and associates (New York: Harper & Brothers, 1936).

This book contains sets of questions to be used in finding out the trade knowledge of applicants for positions in nearly two hundred different occupations.

Aptitudes and Aptitude Testing, by Walter V. Bingham (New York: Harper & Brothers, 1937).

One of the best known and widely used texts on this subject. The technical terms used are defined simply and clearly. No previous training in psychology is assumed.

Appraisal Vocational Fitness by Means of Psychological Tests, by Donald E. Super (New York: Harper & Brothers, 1949).

More than three-fourths of the book is given over to a description and critical analysis of a number of the better known tests.

Wage Incentive Methods, by Charles W. Lytle (New York: The Ronald Press Co.; revised, 1938).

A painstaking and thorough study of the whole problem of wage payment. All the better-known plans are described in considerable detail.

Public Speaking as Listeners Like it, by Richard C. Borden (New York: Harper & Brothers, 1935).

A practical little book of 111 pages, written from the listener's viewpoint; excellent for the executive who does not have time to study one of the longer, more formal texts on this subject.

Industrial Psychology, by Joseph Tiffin (New York: Prentice-Hall, Inc.; revised edition, 1947).

Few, if any, other texts on the general subject of industrial psychology have so much material directly usable by the personnel executive. The chapter on visual skills and vision tests is especially interesting and complete.

INDEX